I0108749

Broken
Chains

Dr. Cassundra White-Elliott

CLF PUBLISHING, LLC.
www.clfpublishing.org
(909) 315-3161

Cover Design by Senir Design. Contact information-info@senirdesign.com.

ISBN # 978-0-9960815-4-2

Printed in the United States of America.

Dedications

This book is dedicated to the broken hearted. God is a healer. And, if you allow Him to, He will heal your wounds, your emotions, your sickness and disease. He will make you anew, in Him. Be blessed!

Acnowledgements

I acknowledge my readers on this project: Rod Flemister and Julia Lary. Thank you for your feedback.

Table of Contents

Introduction

Everyone has dreams and aspirations of living a carefree and painless life. However, the reality of how our life actually turns out is very far from the dream we once held. As we traverse through this journey we call life, we will have the pleasure and sometimes the displeasure of going through an abundance of experiences, and some of the experiences may seem unbearable. Each experience we encounter comes to strengthen us, whether it is a pleasurable one or not.

As we endure each trial and each test, we must always keep in mind nothing happens to us without God knowing about it or without His approval. In the midst of it all, we do not always understand why difficulties and tragedies come across our path or God's intentions. However, if we believe the word of God, we must believe what Romans 8:28 says: *"All things work together for good to those that love God and are called according to his purpose."*

Sometimes we may even find ourselves asking God "Why?" or "Why me?" And we may not get an answer to the question right away or an answer with which we are completely satisfied. But if we trust God, we know that He will not give us more than we can bear, He will not leave us nor forsake us, and He will be with us until the end of the earth. Furthermore, God is not a man that He should lie, and His word will not return unto Him void. It will accomplish that for which it has been sent.

Some of the trials we may endure include, but are not limited to, various types of abuse, promiscuous behaviors, death of loved ones, broken relationships, and afflictions of illness and/or disease.

Women, the world around, have been and continue to be victimized by others. In their homes, women have been beaten, verbally abused, sexually abused, and mentally tormented. And even though the abuse may have occurred years ago, some of the scars still remain today. Those scars have led some women into patterns of promiscuity as they desperately attempt to carve a place for themselves in this world.

Although death is all around us and is an everyday occurrence, it is not the easiest event to bear. We know our loved ones will not always be with us, but at the same time, it is still not easy to say goodbye.

Forging relationships with others is a blessing; however, sometimes there may be a price to pay. Healthy relationships do not come without work, and sometimes they have their ups and downs. However, if both parties are willing they can make the relationship healthy and long lasting.

Along with abuse, promiscuity, death, and broken relationships, some of us endure illness, sickness, and disease. Coming to terms with a medical diagnosis can be unfathomable; however, the Lord God is with us always. He is the great physician, and He has the capability to heal us. And all that we do and all that we encounter, the Lord Jesus Christ should be at the forefront of our mind, for He is our savior, our leader and our guide.

As we march day by day, we will keep our heads uplifted toward the hills from whence cometh our help. Our help cometh from the Lord.

Breaking the Chains of
the effects of
Sexual Abuse

To an educated person, sexual abuse involving children is commonly thought of as incidents that occur in remote areas or amongst people with low educational levels. However, sexual abuse does not have a face, socioeconomic status, gender, or geographic location. Moreover, sexual abuse is not a respecter of persons. Consequently, sexual abuse of children is on the rise and occurs everywhere and, unfortunately, at all times.

According to Sedlak (1996), the incidents of sexual abuse doubled between 1986 and 1993 (quoted in Hodges & Myers, 2010, p. 139). According to the Bureau of Statistics, in 2000, 67% of all sexual assault victims were juveniles, 34% were younger than 12, and about 15% (one in seven) were younger than 6 (quoted in Hodges & Myers, 2010, p. 139). In 2007, the National Center of Victims of Crime reported girls are victimized at least three times more often than boys, and one in four adolescent girls will experience childhood sexual abuse before reaching the age of eighteen (quoted in Hodges & Myers, 2010, p. 139).

After children experience sexual abuse, their lives do not end there. As the saying goes, "Life goes on." Eventually, the children reach adulthood. As the adults struggle to face their personal accounts of sexual abuse that occurred when they were adolescents, mental health counselors notice challenges of self-mutilation, eating disorders, dissociative disorders, and antisocial behavior (Wise, Florio, Benz & Geier, 2007) (quoted in Hodges & Myers, 2010, p. 140). Regardless of the exact nature of the abusive incidents, people who were sexually abused as children may suffer "mental, emotional, relational, and trauma-response issues" (Hodges

& Myers, 2010, p. 141). Each "issue" will be discussed, explained, defined and exemplified below.

Mental Health

As abuse victims go through their lives, they may experience issues with their mental health, to a lesser or higher degree. Issues of *mental health* may include psychiatric disorders and high levels of depression (Hodges & Myers, 2010). There may be times when they may experience situations that will cause them to revisit the abuse they once suffered. The flashbacks and experiences they have may cause them to experience depression as they struggle to understand their overwhelming range of emotions and how to deal with the emotions so their lives are not thrown off kilter. Victims may even wonder why they were victims. The question of why a person is the chosen victim of abuse can only be answered by the abuser, and oftentimes, the abuser cannot answer the question either because something is definitely twisted in the mind of a person who would abuse a child. As a result, the question goes unanswered, and the victims are left with feelings of non-closure.

According to WebMD's Depression Health Center, "Depression is a serious and pervasive mood disorder. It causes feelings of sadness, hopelessness, helplessness, and worthlessness. Depression can be mild to moderate with symptoms of apathy, little appetite, difficulty sleeping, low self-esteem, and low-grade fatigue. Or it can be more severe" (Goldberg, 2013). The National Institute of Mental Health (NIMH), (2014) declares depression, "interferes with daily life and causes pain for both you and those who care about you."

Depression surfaces in many forms:

Major depression—severe symptoms that interfere with your ability to work, sleep, study, eat, and enjoy life. An episode can occur only once in a person's lifetime, but more often, a person has several episodes.

Persistent depressive disorder—depressed mood that lasts for at least two years. A person diagnosed with persistent depressive disorder may have episodes of major depression along with periods of less severe symptoms, but symptoms must last for two years.

Some forms of depression are slightly different, or they may develop under unique circumstances. They include:

Psychotic depression, which occurs when a person has severe depression plus some form of psychosis, such as having disturbing false beliefs or a break with reality (delusions), or hearing or seeing upsetting things that others cannot hear or see (hallucinations).

Postpartum depression, which is much more serious than the "baby blues" that many women experience after giving birth, when hormonal and physical changes and the new responsibility of caring for a newborn can be overwhelming. It is estimated that 10 to 15 percent of women experience postpartum depression after giving birth.

Seasonal affective disorder (SAD), which is characterized by the onset of depression during the winter months, when there is less natural sunlight. The depression generally lifts during spring and summer. SAD may be effectively treated with light therapy, but nearly half of those with SAD do not get better with light therapy alone. Antidepressant medication and psychotherapy can reduce SAD symptoms, either alone or in combination with light therapy.

Bipolar disorder, also called manic-depressive illness, is not as common as major depression or persistent depressive disorder. Bipolar disorder is characterized by cycling mood changes—from extreme highs (e.g., mania) to extreme lows (e.g., depression).
(NIMH, 2014)

"Once diagnosed, a person with depression can be treated in several ways. The most common treatments are medication and psychotherapy," (NIMH, 2014) when operating in the world system. However, those who are spiritually inclined may seek healing from Jehovah Rapha, our God who heals. It is a personal choice how one decides to go about his/her healing. We must note, God has given us doctors and other professionals to consult. At the same time, He is the divine creator, and all power is in His hands. That is true for today, tomorrow, and forever more.

To provide a picture of the devastating effects of depression, read the following account:

Hezekiah, the thirteenth king of Judah, who reigned for twenty-five years, suffered depression when he received word from the prophet Isaiah that he would soon die. Read below Isaiah 38: 1-22. *"In those days Hezekiah became ill and was at the point of death. The prophet Isaiah son of Amoz went to him and said, 'This is what the LORD says: Put your house in order, because you are going to die; you will not recover.' Hezekiah turned his face to the wall and prayed to the LORD, 'Remember, LORD, how I have walked before you faithfully and with wholehearted devotion and have done what is good in your eyes.' And Hezekiah wept bitterly. Then the word of the LORD came to Isaiah: 'Go and tell Hezekiah, "This is what the LORD, the God of your father David, says: I have heard your prayer and seen your tears; I will add fifteen years to your life. And I will deliver you and this city from the hand of the king of Assyria. I will defend this city.*

'This is the LORD's sign to you that the LORD will do what he has promised: I will make the shadow cast by the sun go back the ten steps it has gone down on the stairway of Ahaz.'" So the sunlight went back the ten steps it had gone down. A writing of Hezekiah king of Judah after his illness and recovery: I said, 'In the prime of my life must I go through the gates of death and be robbed of the rest of my years?' I said, 'I will not again see the LORD himself in the land of the living; no longer will I look on my fellow man, or be with those who now dwell in this world. Like a shepherd's tent my house has been pulled down and taken from me. Like a weaver I have rolled up my life, and he has cut me off from the loom; day and night you made an end of me. I waited patiently till dawn, but like a lion he broke all my bones; day and night you made an end of me. I cried like a swift or thrush, I moaned like a mourning dove. My eyes grew weak as I looked to the heavens. I am being threatened; Lord, come to my aid!' But what can I say? He has spoken to me, and he himself has done this. I will walk humbly all my years because of this anguish of

my soul. Lord, by such things people live; and my spirit finds life in them too. You restored me to health and let me live. Surely it was for my benefit that I suffered such anguish. In your love you kept me from the pit of destruction; you have put all my sins behind your back. For the grave cannot praise you, death cannot sing your praise; those who go down to the pit cannot hope for your faithfulness. The living, the living—they praise you, as I am doing today; parents tell their children about your faithfulness. The LORD will save me, and we will sing with stringed instruments all the days of our lives in the temple of the LORD. Isaiah had said, 'Prepare a poultice of figs and apply it to the boil, and he will recover.' Hezekiah had asked, 'What will be the sign that I will go up to the temple of the LORD?'"

Sometime after hearing the prophetic words of the prophet Isaiah, Hezekiah "turned his face toward the wall and wept bitterly" because he felt he was going to be robbed of the rest of his earthly life while only being in his prime. However, it is important to take notice he did not plead with God to spare his life, nor did he try to tie the hand of God by bargaining with Him to extend his life because of the deeds he had done. Instead, his only request was for God to remember the work he had done in His name. God heard Hezekiah's cry, and added fifteen years to his life. Isaiah's prophecy was revoked.

Although Hezekiah's case of depression did not stem from sexual abuse, there is much we can earn from Hezekiah and his experience with depression, a deep feeling of helplessness. First, the depth of depression Hezekiah suffered was of the same magnitude abuse victims suffer.

Second, regardless of the cause of the depression, Hezekiah needed a healthy reprieve, as does abuse victims.

Other biblical figures who suffered depression include Abraham, when he believed he would die childless (Genesis 15); Jonah, the prophet, who walked in disobedience to God when he was instructed to declare the words of the Lord in the land of Nineveh (Joshua 4); Job, when he lost his family and his possessions (Book of Job); Elijah, when he ran for his life from Ahab and Jezebel (1 Kings 19); King Saul, when the spirit of the Lord departed from him (1 Samuel 16:14-23); Cain, after slaying his brother (Genesis 4:6-7).

Just as people during the Bible times suffered depression, believers and non-believers alike have the capacity to suffer depression. However, it is not God's will for us to be emotionally unbalanced. Therefore, should any person suffer from severe depression, abuse victim or not, he/she should seek healing.

Some scriptures that can help one to prevent or deal with bouts of depression are:

- *"Why art thou cast down, O my soul? and why art thou disquieted in me? hope thou in God: for I shall yet praise him for the help of his countenance. For thou art the God of my strength: why dost thou cast me off? why go I mourning because of the oppression of the enemy."* (Psalm 42:5, 43:2 KJV).
- *"Trust in the LORD with all your heart, And lean not on your own understanding; In all your ways acknowledge Him, And He shall direct your paths"* (Proverbs 3:5-6 NKJV).

17

- *"Now may the God of hope fill you with all joy and peace in believing, that you may abound in hope by the power of the Holy Spirit" (Romans 15:13 NKJV).*
- *"Rejoice in the Lord always. Again I will say, rejoice! Let your gentleness be known to all men. The Lord is at hand. Be anxious for nothing, but in everything by prayer and supplication, with thanksgiving, let your requests be made known to God; and the peace of God, which surpasses all understanding, will guard your hearts and minds through Christ Jesus. Finally, brethren, whatever things are true, whatever things are noble, whatever things are just, whatever things are pure, whatever things are lovely, whatever things are of good report, if there is any virtue and if there is anything praiseworthy; meditate on these things" (Philippians 4:4-8 NKJV).*
- *"Therefore humble yourselves under the mighty hand of God, that He may exalt you in due time, casting all your care upon Him, for He cares for you" (1 Peter 5:6-7).*
- *"We are hard pressed on every side, yet not crushed; we are perplexed, but not in despair; persecuted, but not forsaken; struck down, but not destroyed... Therefore we do not lose heart. Though outwardly we are wasting away, yet inwardly we are being renewed day by day. For our light and momentary troubles are achieving for us an eternal glory that far outweighs them all. So we fix our eyes not on what is seen, but on what is unseen. For what is seen is temporary, but what is unseen is eternal" (2 Corinthians 4:8-9, 16-18 NIV).*

Emotional Health

Let us shift gears from mental health to *emotional health*. According to psychologist Dr. Shannon Kolakowski (2013), when one is emotionally healthy, he/she embodies the following seven characteristics/behavior traits:

1. *You treat others well.* Viewing other people with compassion and treating them with kindness is a hallmark of your own well-being. Psychologists call this *prosociality*. It means you tend to be sensitive to the needs and feelings of other people, and you think it's important to help others. It's basically the idea that you'll lend a hand to someone in need -- even if it's as simple as returning a lost wallet to the front desk of a hotel lobby, or smiling and making friendly conversation with the person standing next to you in line.

2. *You like who you are.* When you're emotionally healthy, you generally feel pretty good about who you are. You know yourself -- foibles, quirks and strengths and you're okay with what's inside. You're also congruent: congruency means that the person you show to the outside world is reflective of who you are on the inside. While there are situations where you naturally shift your attitude or behavior a bit depending on the social situation (i.e., it's normal to behave differently at a work luncheon then at a weekend picnic with friends), congruence means your overall sense of who you are feels in line with what you show others. It's the opposite of feeling like you have to wear a mask or pretend to be someone you're not. Instead, you're able to be genuine with yourself and others. You feel like you're living the life you want, not living the life that others want you to have.

3. *You're flexible.* People who have emotional wellness have an ability to adapt to all kinds of situations that life throws at us. You're able to assess a situation mindfully -- you notice your surroundings, your emotions and other's reactions to a given situation -- and then you use these factors to decide what the best course of action is. With colleagues, friendships, or your kids, flexibility is knowing that sometimes you need to talk things out, and sometimes it's best to let a situation cool off. You stand up for yourself when need be, but you're also able let others have the last word. You know how to have tough conversations and set boundaries, but you also know when to let things go. You approach life and relationships with an openness and sense of curiosity, knowing that you might need to adjust your course of action when one strategy isn't working. Flexibility is the core component of current psychological treatments because it allows you to make decisions based on your values and to make choices that will serve you well in life.

4. *You hold gratitude for your loved ones.* If you're emotionally healthy, it's likely you easily feel and show gratitude for the people and the things in your life. Holding gratitude is a way of purposefully looking at your life with a sense of appreciation for what you have, rather than focusing on what you are lacking. And indeed, research has shown that counting your blessings has strong benefits for emotional well-being. Showing appreciation for your loved ones is a key factor in relationship well-being. When you show gratitude, it means that your husband or wife, your kids, your parents -- the people who matter to you -- know you love them and feel valued by you. It doesn't mean you don't fight or say things you regret at times, and it doesn't

mean you will always have the perfect relationship. But when it comes down to it, you're able to show unconditional love and affection for your family. You give hugs, warmth, appreciation and attention freely, and you share in your triumphs together. Next, emotional well-being depends on your receiving social support. We all need a nurturing, loving environment to thrive. This means you have people you can depend on, friends and family who have your best interest at heart. In your relationships, you feel safe to express how you feel and you feel respected and validated by those closest to you.

5. *You're in touch with your emotions.* Another sign of emotional wellness is that you embrace your emotions -- sadness, anger, anxiety, joy, fear, and excitement -- as a natural and normal part of life. You handle and acknowledge your difficult emotions without becoming overwhelmed by them or by denying that your emotions exist. You know it's normal to have periods of stress, you know how to manage and express yourself when you feel upset, and you know whom you can go to get comfort or help. Your feelings of sadness, anxiety and fears -- while acknowledged -- also aren't getting in the way of what you love to do. So if you're afraid of flying or public speaking, you manage to take the flight or give the speech regardless. Emotional health comes from being able to label, acknowledge and accept tough emotions, but also move forward from them without getting stuck. This means you might get nervous before going on date, but you don't let the nerves stop you from going out altogether.

At the same time, savoring your positive emotions -- reveling in those moments of pleasure, happiness and joy when they come your way -- is also linked to well-being.

6. *You have meaning in your life.* Leading a purposeful life is about having a passion, a mission or larger meaning to your life. This happens when you use your strengths to help something you believe in. It might be volunteering with kids, being involved in politics, being an active part of your religious group, contributing to your neighborhood or child's school, or competing in a marathon or triathlon for a good cause. Regardless of the cause, being part of something you connect with and care about is largely associated with well-being, and volunteerism is even associated with living a longer life.

7. *You value experiences more than possessions.* The final component is considering the types of values you have in life. People who tend to highly value attaining wealth, popularity, or attractiveness tend to be less well-off emotionally than people who value self-fulfillment and being there for others. This means that while you might have goals for career and financial security, you also may highly value time with your family and friends. Additionally, people with high levels of well-being tend to spend their money on experiences, like going to a concert or going on a trip, rather than material possessions such as clothes or furniture. Experiences may be more meaningful than possessions because they lead to shared experiences and bonding with people, help you enjoy the beauty in the world and cultivate the positive emotions that come with new experiences.

On the other hand, issues of emotional health include "social mal-adjustments, self-blame, anger, low self-esteem, self-destruction, and anxiety" (Kessler, White, & Nelson, 2003; Ulman, 2006) (quoted in Hodges & Myers, 2010, p. 141). Women survivors are likely to experience challenges in five major areas of emotional functioning: trust, safety, intimacy, self-esteem and control (Shipherd, Street, & Resick, 2006) (quoted in Hodges & Myers, 2010, p. 141). These resulting issues may stem from emotional abuse.

Gregory Jantz, a popular psychologist, speaker, and radio personality in Seattle, Washington, defines emotional abuse as, "the consistent pattern of being treated unfairly and unjustly over a period of time, usually by the same person or people. It can also, be a onetime traumatic event that is left unresolved" (12).

According to the Good Therapy Foundation (2014),

Trust- the act of placing confidence in someone or something else- is a fundamental human experience, necessary for society to function and for any person to be relatively happy. Without it, fear rules. Trust is not an either/or proposition, but a matter of degree, and certain life experiences can impact a person's ability to trust others. Everyone has uncertainty about whom to trust, how much to trust, when not to trust, and so forth at one time or another. In fact, every day we make choices about whom and how much to trust, and sometimes we are more willing to trust than at other times. That's a good thing; a total lack of mistrust would indicate a serious psychological problem. Judgments about when and whom to trust help keep us safe and alive!

Signs that a person may be excessively mistrustful include:

- A total lack of intimacy or friendships due to mistrust
- Mistrust that interferes with one's primary relationship
- Several intensely dramatic and stormy relationships in a row or at once
- Racing thoughts of suspicion or anxiety about friends and family
- Terror during physical intimacy
- Belief that others are deceptive and malevolent, without real evidence

When mistrust seems to play a dominant role in a person's life, past disappointments or betrayals may be at the root of the issue. Mistrust is a valid and reasoned response to feeling betrayed or abandoned, but a person's life can be adversely affected when feelings of mistrust are pervasive, resulting in anxiety, anger, or self-doubt. Fortunately, a person can learn to trust again, and working with a therapist can aid this process.

From a spiritual perspective, the word of God says, "I have not given you the spirit of fear, but of love, power, and a sound mind." Fear is an emotion that is rendered from Satan and oftentimes leads to mistrust. When a person embodies mistrust that mistrust may flow over into his/her spiritual relationship with the heavenly father. Amos 3:3 (KJV) says, *"Can two walk together, except they be agreed?"* So, if one person does not trust another and vice versa, how can they complete a task or be in a relationship? The same is true for our relationship with God. If we do not trust His word, we will be unable to commune with Him fully and will forfeit the benefits we have as a child of God. To develop our trust in God is simply to develop our faith. Faith development………

Psalms 27 declares, *"The LORD is my light and my salvation; whom shall I fear? the LORD is the strength of my life; of whom shall I be afraid? When the wicked, even mine enemies and my foes, came upon me to eat up my flesh, they stumbled and fell. Though an host should encamp against me, my heart shall not fear: though war should rise against me, in this will I be confident. One thing have I desired of the LORD, that will I seek after; that I may dwell in the house of the LORD all the days of my life, to behold the beauty of the LORD, and to enquire in his temple. For in the time of trouble he shall hide me in his pavilion: in the secret of his tabernacle shall he hide me; he shall set me up upon a rock. And now shall mine head be lifted up above mine enemies round about me: therefore will I offer in his tabernacle sacrifices of joy; I will sing, yea, I will sing praises unto the LORD."*

The Bible includes 385 scriptures on fear that explain why we should 'fear not.' Included below are fifty of those scriptures from various versions of the Bible. To read the collection of all 385 scriptures about fear and an explanation for each, get a copy of my book *Fear Not*. It will truly assist in eradicating unhealthy fears from your life.

1. *For God has not given us a spirit of fear and timidity, but of power, love, and self-discipline* (2 Timothy 1:7 NLT).

2. *Do not be afraid, little flock, for your Father has been pleased to give you the kingdom* (Luke 12:32 NIV).

3. *The angel of the LORD encamps around those who fear him, and he delivers them* (Psalm 34:7 NIV).

4. *So don't be afraid; you are worth more than many sparrows* (Matt 10:31 NIV).

5. *Serve only the Lord your God and fear him alone. Obey his commands, listen to his voice, and cling to him* (Deuteronomy 13:4 NLT).

6. *I am leaving you with a gift—peace of mind and heart. And the peace I give is a gift the world cannot give. So don't be troubled or afraid* (John 14:27 NLT).

7. *This is my command—be strong and courageous! Do not be afraid or discouraged. For the Lord your God is with you wherever you go* (Joshua 1:9 NLT).

8. *But even if you suffer for doing what is right, God will reward you for it. So don't worry or be afraid of their threats* (1 Peter 3:14 NLT).

9. *One night the Lord spoke to Paul in a vision and told him, "Don't be afraid! Speak out! Don't be silent!"* (Acts 18:9 NLT).

10. *Such love has no fear, because perfect love expels all fear. If we are afraid, it is for fear of punishment, and this shows that we have not fully experienced his perfect love* (1 John 4:18 NLT).

11. *When I am afraid, I put my trust in you* (Psalm 56:3 NIV).

12. *In God, whose word I praise- in God I trust and am not afraid. What can mere mortals do to me?* (Psalm 56:4 NIV).

13. *He will cover you with his feathers. He will shelter you with his wings. His faithful promises are your armor and protection. Do not be afraid of the terrors of the night, nor the arrow that flies in the day. Do not dread the disease that stalks in darkness, nor the disaster that strikes at midday. Though a thousand fall at your side, though ten thousand are dying around you, these evils will not touch you* (Psalm 91:4-8 NLT).

14. *They do not fear bad news; they confidently trust the Lord to care for them* (Psalm 112:7 NLT).

15. *Do not tremble; do not be afraid. Did I not proclaim my purposes for you long ago? You are my witnesses—is there any other God? No! There is no other Rock—not one!* (Isaiah 44:8 NLT).

16. *I am the one who comforts you. So why are you afraid of mere humans, who wither like the grass and disappear?* (Isaiah 51:12 NLT).

17. *Be not afraid of them [their faces], for I am with you to deliver you, says the* Lord (Jeremiah 1:8 Amplified).

18. *But Jesus overheard them and said to Jairus, "Don't be afraid. Just have faith"* (Mark 5:36 NLT).

19. *They had rowed three or four miles when suddenly they saw Jesus walking on the water toward the boat. They were terrified, but he called out to them, "Don't be afraid. I am here!"* (John 6:19-20 NLT).

20. *"Don't be afraid," Moses answered them, "for God has come in this way to test you, and so that your fear of him will keep you from sinning!"* (Exodus 20:20 NLT).

21. *You must always act in the fear of the Lord, with faithfulness and an undivided heart* (2 Chronicles 19:9 NLT).
22. *The Lord is a friend to those who fear him. He teaches them his covenant* (Psalm 25:14 NLT).
23. *But the Lord watches over those who fear him, those who rely on his unfailing love* (Psalm 33:18 NLT).
24. *I prayed to the Lord, and he answered me. He freed me from all my fears* (Psalm 34:4 NLT).
25. *Fear the Lord, you his godly people, for those who fear him will have all they need* (Psalm 34:9 NLT).
26. *The Lord is like a father to his children, tender and compassionate to those who fear him* (Psalm 103:13 NLT).
27. *Fear of the Lord leads to life, bringing security and protection from harm* (Proverbs 19:23 NLT).
28. *True humility and fear of the Lord lead to riches, honor, and long life* (Proverbs 22:4 NLT).
29. *Fearing people is a dangerous trap, but trusting the Lord means safety* (Proverbs 29:25 NLT).
30. *Charm is deceptive, and beauty does not last; but a woman who fears the Lord will be greatly praised* (Proverbs 31:30 NLT).
31. *He will be your sure foundation, providing a rich store of salvation, wisdom, and knowledge. The fear of the Lord will be your treasure* (Isaiah 33:6 NLT).
32. *Say to those with fearful hearts, "Be strong, and do not fear, for your God is coming to destroy your enemies. He is coming to save you"* (Isaiah 35:4 NLT).
33. *Listen to me, you who know right from wrong you who cherish my law in your hearts. Do not be afraid*

of people's scorn, nor fear their insults (Isaiah 51:7 NLT).

34. *Fear not; you will no longer live in shame. Don't be afraid; there is no more disgrace for you. You will no longer remember the shame of your youth and the sorrows of widowhood* (Isaiah 54:4 NLT).

35. *For the Lord your God is living among you. He is a mighty savior. He will take delight in you with gladness. With his love, he will calm all your fears. He will rejoice over you with joyful songs* (Zephaniah 3:17 NLT).

36. *Don't be afraid of those who want to kill your body; they cannot touch your soul. Fear only God, who can destroy both soul and body in hell* (Matt 10:28 NLT).

37. *We have been rescued from our enemies so we can serve God without fear, in holiness and righteousness for as long as we live* (Luke 1:74-75 NLT).

38. *And I am convinced that nothing can ever separate us from God's love. Neither death nor life, neither angels nor demons, neither our fears for today nor our worries about tomorrow—not even the powers of hell can separate us from God's love* (Romans 8:38 NLT).

39. *We faced conflict from every direction, with battles on the outside and fear on the inside. But God, who encourages those who are discouraged, encouraged us by the arrival of Titus. His presence was a joy* (2 Corinthians 7:5-6 NLT).

40. *Since we are receiving a Kingdom that is unshakable, let us be thankful and please God by worshiping him with holy fear and awe* (Hebrews 12:28 NLT).

41. *Such love has no fear, because perfect love expels all fear. If we are afraid, it is for fear of punishment, and this shows that we have not fully experienced his perfect love* (1 John 4:18 NLT).
42. *"Fear God," he shouted. "Give glory to him. For the time has come when he will sit as judge. Worship him who made the heavens, the earth, the sea, and all the springs of water"* (Revelation 14:7 NLT)
43. *And from the throne came a voice that said, "Praise our God, all his servants, all who fear him, from the least to the greatest"* (Revelation 19:5 NLT).
44. *Even though I walk through the darkest valley, I will fear no evil, for you are with* me (Psalm 23:4 NIV).
45. *Do not be afraid of anyone, for judgment belongs to God* (Deuteronomy 1:17 NIV).
46. *Do not be afraid of them; the LORD your God himself will fight for* you (Deuteronomy 3:22 NIV).
47. *The LORD is my light and my salvation— whom shall I fear? The LORD is the stronghold of my life— of whom shall I be afraid?* (Psalm 27:1 NIV).
48. *He said to his disciples, "Why are you so afraid? Do you still have no faith?"* (Mark 4:40 NIV)
49. *Jesus told him, "Don't be afraid; just believe"* (Mark 5:36 NIV).
50. *Then he placed his right hand on me and said: "Do not be afraid. I am the First and the Last* (Revelation 1:17 NIV).

Now that we have thoroughly examined the effects of mistrust, let us examine the benefits of having "healthy trust" in our lives. To exemplify this concept, I will illustrate a biblical account from the book of Joshua.

After Joshua and the Israelite troops quietly marched around the city of Jericho six times and gave a great shout on the seventh rotation, causing the walls to come down, they seized the city. Once inside the city, only the harlot Rahab and the inhabitants in her house were spared. You may ask, "Why was Rahab spared? As a harlot, wasn't she a sinner?" Rahab was a non-believer and a prostitute. Yes, she was a sinner. However, when she learned of the Israelites and their god and all He had carried them through (through the Red Sea and through difficulties with kings, whom they were able to defeat), she knew their god was with them and would give them possession of the city of Jericho. She knew their god was powerful, for she stated, "For the LORD your God is God in heaven above and on the earth below" (Joshua 2:11b).

Prior to the actual seizing of Jericho, Joshua sent two spies to go into Jericho to scout the land. While they were there, they went to Rahab's house, and she hid them to keep them safe. Upon their departure, she made a request of the two spies that she and her house be spared upon the Israelites' return to seize the city. Although her lifestyle was not pleasing unto God, because she kept God's men safe, her request was granted. Rahab trusted the spies' word that if she hung the scarlet rope down her wall, she and her family would be spared, if they remained inside her home.

These men were strangers to Rahab, but something about them and their god made her believe she could trust them. Having a healthy amount of trust and using your spiritual discernment will do wonders in your life. If Rahab had not trusted the men and made her appeal unto them, she would have perished with the rest of Jericho.

Who is your trust in today?

Relational Issues

In addition to mental and emotional distress, sexual abuse has yet another effect: It is one of the leading causes of relationship issues, specifically in male/female relationships. Relational issues can result regardless of the relationship between the victim and the abuser. Sometimes the victim knows the abuser, while in other cases, he/she does not. However, when there is a personal relationship between the abuser and abused, the effects tend to be exponentially worse. When a person (family member, church member, school official) who is connected to another person and uses their relationship to sexually abuse him/her, the abuse can lead to future relational issues. For example, when a person whom children trust abuses them, the children tend to develop trust issues that impact their future relationships. Take the case of King David's daughter Tamar.

King David and Maacah bore two children together: a son, Absalom and a daughter, Tamar. Both children were known for their extreme beauty. Tamar was so beautiful that she had to be escorted everywhere she went because men were very taken with her. She was never out of her servants' sight. However, her half-brother

Amnon (one of David's sons) had a strange and unnatural affinity for his half-sister. He actually lusted after her and desired to have her for himself.

In those days, it may have been permissible for Amnon to ask their father, King David, for Tamar's hand in marriage. But instead of going that route, he decided to take matters into his own hands. He and one of his servants concocted a plan to lure Tamar into Amnon's bedchambers. The pretense given was Amnon was extremely ill. After doctors examined him and could not offer any treatments, David was extremely concerned, for he loved all of his sons dearly.

At his son's request, David permitted Tamar to cook her brother food and take it into his chambers. And as was the custom, Tamar's servants accompanied her. Amnon was quite adamant about getting her alone, so he feigned craziness and demanded everyone to leave the room. At his request, every person departed. He then summoned his sister over to his bedside to feed him as he demonstrated an inability to feed himself. As Tamar reached in to feed her supposedly ailing brother, he grabbed her. His actions and the look in his eyes revealed to her what he had in mind. She physically resisted him and told him they could marry if he desired and begged him not to do what he was attempting to do. Her refusal was to no avail. Amnon raped his sister and then suddenly turned against her. With great disdain, Amnon called for his servant and demanded he take Tamar out of his chambers. He went from lusting after her to not being able to stand the sight of her. Tamar wept loudly and placed ashes upon her head.

She eventually made her way to the royal harem, and what had befallen her became knowledge throughout the family. Her father King David did nothing to right the wrong, but two years later, her brother Absalom avenged his sister by having their half-brother Amnon murdered.

Can you imagine the way Tamar must have felt after being violated by someone she loved and trusted? This is how so many victims feel when their trust is betrayed. Not only was Tamar betrayed by her brother, but she was also neglected by their father King David who did nothing about the rape. She was left to live the rest of her life with the shame that was brought to her family over an incident of which she had no control. This incident of betrayal within the family caused a great rift by turning brother against sister (Amnon/Tamar), sister against father (Tamar/King David), and son against father (Absalom/King David), and brother against brother (Absalom/Amnon).

Now, let us examine an incident of sexual abuse from a total stranger. This case study was shared by psychotherapist Peter A. Carich (2001) in his article titled, "Use of Adlerian Concepts in Healing Severe Physical and Sexual Abuse."

When I first met Camille, she was a 22-year-old, unmarried White woman who lived at home with her parents and attended college part-time while working full-time. She had graduated from high school with honors. She had been active in high school and had participated in social and athletic activities. At the time, Camille had been working as a receptionist for an insurance company for three years and had completed two years of college. She had not experienced any severe illnesses or trauma prior to her being sexually assaulted. She did not smoke and rarely drank alcoholic beverages. Her health had been excellent. She was well-groomed, and she did not appear hostile or angry. Her motor activity was normal, and she appeared well-coordinated. There was no evidence of tics or any peculiar mannerisms.

The traumatic event. Camille had been referred for psychotherapy after recuperating in a hospital following a brutal physical and sexual attack. The whole traumatic episode had lasted about 18 hours. She had spent three weeks in the hospital. Upon discharge from the hospital, her physicians immediately referred her for psychotherapy.

Camille's traumatic episode began around noon as she was going to work. Her automobile had stalled near a very busy intersection, and she had been unable to get it started. She had been only a few blocks from work. A driver of a small business truck had stopped, parked behind her automobile, and offered to help her. He could not get it started; therefore, he offered her a ride to the nearest repair shop. She declined, but he kept on insisting, and finally he persuaded her to get into the truck. Everything appeared normal except that when they were near the repair garage, he picked up speed and turned toward the interstate. She knew at that moment she was in trouble and helpless. She questioned the driver, and he responded by telling her to keep her mouth shut. He drove for several hours to a secluded cabin in a wooded area. He raped and sodomized her repeatedly and beat her when she resisted his sexual activities. After midnight, he drove her back to a densely wooded area near the place where the whole episode began. She could hear automobiles, so she realized that they were near a highway. The sexual abuse continued in the truck and in the wooded area.

At approximately 3:00 A.M., Camille's assailant stabbed her in the chest seven times. After being stabbed, Camille dropped to the ground and acted as if she were dead. She felt a burning sensation and some blood. She was fortunate in that no vital organs and arteries were punctured. Because it was dark, the attacker thought she was dead as she lay on the ground. He took some leaves and covered her, and then went back to his truck, parked about 60 feet away. She heard him start the truck, but she was too afraid to move. He took a gun from the truck and shot into the pile of leaves. The bullet grazed her arm. Soon it sounded like he left, but she lay still in the leaves for two more hours before trying to move. She was extremely weak from the loss of blood, and the night was cold. At about 6:00 AM, she struggled to the highway. A worker from a nearby hospital was going to work, and put her in his automobile and took her to the hospital, which was less than a mile away. She was immediately rushed into surgery and discharged three weeks later.

Diagnosis and psychotherapy. As a result of the traumatic experience, Camille was suffering from recurring recollections of the horror of the abuse, fear, and initial and terminal insomnia. She also had feelings of inferiority, low self-worth, feelings of inadequacy, mixed emotions, some difficulty in concentrating, and guilt over trusting a stranger and allowing the sexual acts to go on even though realistically she did not have any choice.

Psychotherapy began with my working to establish a relationship consisting of trust, empathy, understanding, acceptance, and good rapport. By the second session, she was able to reveal the explicit details of what had been done to her and had caused a severe upheaval in her life. In sessions three and four, I conveyed to her that because she was conscious and aware of what took place, these stressful negative feelings should be expected. At the same time, I stressed the importance of reconciling this traumatic event emotionally. She must realize that the event will never go away but once reconciled will end up being a historical event that took place in her life with no feelings attached to it.

In sessions five and six, I emphasized the importance of taking control of her future and not allowing this event to control her life. I reassured her that the person she had been before the physical, mental, and sexual abuse was definitely the same person she was here and now. She began to understand that her potential and positive characteristics were still there, but she had to choose to use them instead of punishing herself any further.

In sessions seven and eight, her faulty idea that life should be fair was challenged as she reached an understanding that there are some bad things that go on in society. I suggested that overall most people are caring and good as evidenced by the worker who took her to the hospital without concern for his automobile becoming bloody and muddy. Her faulty assumptions about herself, based on the trauma, were challenged.

After several sessions, Camille began to recognize that her positive attributes were still intact, and she began combating her negative self-concepts. I provided her with encouragement and thereby helped her to overcome feelings of discouragement and enabled her to restore her perception of self with dignity, self-worth, and self-respect. The event was desensitized, and she was able to detach herself from the event even though she will never forget it.

The actual gist of the therapeutic approach in sessions seven and eight consisted of encouraging the development of self-understanding and helping Camille make choices through fictional finalism. This term refers to an imagined central goal that guides Camille's behavior. I encouraged Camille to close her eyes and concentrate on forming an image of herself with all of her desirable traits and characteristics as before the traumatic event in her life. As soon as these images were in place, I asked her to wish the time sequence to here and now. I asked her to communicate this image to me. At that point, Camille began to realize that she was the same person that she was before the traumatic event and that none of these positive characteristics have been taken from her. I asked Camille to reveal these characteristics to me in detail. Camille accomplished her goal of reconciliation of the event that had traumatized her life. I reinforced her positive self-image several times in sessions seven and eight by having her list these characteristics on paper. Then, I asked Camille to look at her list several times each day to remind herself of her true self-image.

Summary

The therapist must make sure that the patient does not become dependent on him or her. The reconciliation of the traumatic event faulty perception of self and all other ill feelings must be worked out in small steps so that the patient can grasp the input and make positive changes in his or her life.

Therapy was accomplished by using Adlerian basic principles combined with elements of Existential Theory. Camille's therapy consisted of eight sessions over a three-month period. Upon completion of therapy, Camille was able to deal with life in a more positive way.

Whether or not a woman is sexually abused by a person with whom she is familiar or by a complete stranger, the effects can be long lasting, as we witnessed in the biblical account of King David's daughter Tamar and in Camille's account. The immediate effects of the trauma can lead to specific relational issues, such as low sexual desire and arousal and/or the inability to tolerate touch.

"An adult survivor of child sexual abuse cannot be categorized in any [particular] way, such are the complex dynamics and deep trauma at work in this situation. Generally speaking, adults will normally have one of two postures towards life after such abuse, they will either collapse or they will attempt to rise above the abuse. The collapsed outcome is an adult who often has easily recognizable symptoms and problems that stop them from being functional in one or more areas of their life, often with depressive, or addictive, or victim status personas, or require ongoing medical assistance to cope with life. The second outcome where one "rises above the abuse and its shame" is nominally one who dissociates from the abuse trauma, soldiers on and is able to maintain for some time an intact functional life in work and social settings, but who often withdraws or has impairment issues in intimate relationships" (Boyd, 2010).

"Maltz (2002) suggests that a first step in sexual healing is to help [survivors] connect their current sexual problems with their past sexual abuse. It may help for the survivor to see a list of the sexual symptoms that often are from past sexual abuse. Ratican (1992) describes the sexual symptoms of survivors to often include sexualizing relationships, inappropriate seduction, difficulties with affection and intimacy, compulsive sexual behavior, promiscuity, problems concerning desire, arousal, and orgasm, flashbacks, difficulties with touch, and sadistic/masochistic tendencies" (as cited in American Counseling Association, 2011).

"A treatment designed for sexual healing often focuses on understanding how the sexual abuse influenced their sexuality, adjusting sexual attitudes, gaining a more positive sexual self-concept, decreasing negative sexual behaviors, learning how to cope with negative reactions to touch, and developing skills to positively experience touch and sexual intimacy (Maltz, 2002)" (as cited in American Counseling Association, 2011).

Sexual abuse of children or adult women has "significant and pervasive impact[s] on individuals, producing a variety of mental, emotional, relational, physical, and trauma symptoms. Most therapeutic interventions for sexual abuse focus primarily on reliving or retelling, in great detail, the sexual abuse experience. However, many clients lack a positive sense of self, an internal locus of control, and an ability to view the abuse as only part of who they are rather than the defining elements (Hodges & Myers, 2010, p. 150). Therefore, "a wellness-based intervention" program facilitated by mental health professionals "may increase self-efficacy, resiliency, and awareness of healthy coping skills, resulting in positive changes in everyday functioning" (Hodges & Myers, 2010, p. 150).

Moreover, a mental health professional who is spiritually led, with the guidance and assistance of the Holy Spirit, may assist women in achieving mental, emotional, and relational relief. This relief will effectuate the production of women who can then be instrumental in their own personal lives, the lives of their children and families, and in their churches and communities. Remember, Proverbs 27:3 says, "As a man thinketh, so is he." This tells us what we think will have the greatest impact on our lives. If we believe the lies of the devil, we will carry them out and perform them in our lives. Conversely, if we believe we are to blame for the abuse we suffered, we will continue to torture ourselves and live a sub-standard life. If we see ourselves as victims, we will seek out that role and make ourselves susceptible to abuse. We have choices in life, and it would do us well to exercise those choices. Doing so can lead to healthy relationships.

Breaking the Chains of

Promiscuity

Promiscuous is defined by dictionary.com as "involving indiscriminate mingling or association, especially having sexual relations with a number of partners on a casual basis." Promiscuous behavior can be a result of past sexual abuse one suffered as a child or as an adult. When a woman, who was abused as a child or as an adult, becomes sexually active, some of the choices she makes that involve sexual intercourse may not be the same choices she would have made had she not been abused. "Instead of a loving bond between a man and a woman that we have been designed for, that physical union becomes marred with painful memories. How an individual reacts and copes to being exposed to a sexual relationship before she was mature enough to understand and handle it will vary from person to person. Having been violated, often repeatedly against her will, teaches a child that sex is not about love; it is about being used and often treated as an object" (Healing in the Hurting Places (HHP), 2014).

When a woman is raped, her personal choice to have sexual relations is taken away from her. A woman has the choice to have sex with whom she pleases. However, that choice is stripped from her when a man decides to have sex with her against her will. During the horrific act of rape, some women's virginity is taken. Virginity is something that can only be "lost" once. When women lose their virginity by force or are forced to have sex against their will (virgin or not), oftentimes something clicks within the women, and they begin to feel powerless. The feeling of powerlessness can leave them with a desire to take back the power that was usurped from them.

To regain the usurped power, some women will begin a string of illicit affairs. Having the affairs causes them to feel powerful. With their right to choose, they believe they regain their power. However, as we will discuss later in the chapter, there are other feelings associated with promiscuity, and these feelings override the short-lived feelings of power.

While some women live promiscuous lives, "other victims go in the opposite direction, avoiding sex entirely" (HHP, 2014). The reasons for the different choices varies from one woman to another. On one hand, the woman gives permission to whom she wants to have it when it comes to touching her body. On the other hand, another woman may retain her sense of control by not allowing anyone to touch her (HPP).

"For women who go on to marry, the sexual act can prove troublesome. Certain smells, positions, behaviors or words can trigger repressed or unhealed memories. An older adolescent, whose body responded physically during the act of abuse, may have trouble achieving or sustaining an orgasm, due to guilty feelings over how her body responded previously. Sexual abuse survivors may also not fully enjoy the sexual act during marriage because their minds have become so conditioned to disengaging during sex as a means of being able to mentally survive what was happening to them as children" (HHP).

In our modern society, as well as in times of the past, women have been/are continuing to be victimized and have acted/are acting out as a result. Through different mediums, they strive to regain control over their bodies and over their lives. When we encounter a woman who is promiscuous, we should be very careful not to judge because we do not know what path she has walked upon. And, we definitely do not know the pain she endured and may continue to bear.

One biblical example of promiscuous living that continues to be well known throughout the ages is the story of Mary Magdalene, a prostitute. In the book of John 8:2-11, the following account is shared:

> At dawn he appeared again in the temple courts, where all the people gathered around him, and he sat down to teach them. The teachers of the law and the Pharisees brought in a woman caught in adultery. They made her stand before the group and said to Jesus, "Teacher, this woman was caught in the act of adultery. In the Law Moses commanded us to stone such women. Now what do you say?" They were using this question as a trap, in order to have a basis for accusing him. But Jesus bent down and started to write on the ground with his finger. When they kept on questioning him, he straightened up and said to them, "Let any one of you who is without sin be the first to throw a stone at her." Again he stooped down and wrote on the ground. At this, those who heard began to go away one at a time, the older ones first, until only Jesus was left, with the woman still standing there. Jesus straightened up and asked her, "Woman, where are they? Has no one condemned you?" "No one, sir," she said. "Then neither do I condemn you," Jesus declared. "Go now and leave your life of sin" (NIV).

Mary Magdalene's full story is not shared in the Bible. We do not know how, when, or why she became a prostitute. What we do know is this: prostitutes live a promiscuous life. It is a by-product of the trade. And because promiscuity is a bi-product, prostitutes, as well as other women who live or have lived promiscuous lives, must come to terms with their brokenness in order to be made whole. In most twelve-step programs, the first step is to admit there is a problem.

To exemplify how one can come to terms with her brokenness, recently "Vanessa Williams [began to share] more details about the molestation she suffered at age 10 – and the impact it had on her growing up. 'I think it made me more sexually promiscuous and more sexually curious at a younger age than I should have been,' the actress and former Miss America says in a new episode of *Oprah's Master Class*, which aired Sunday. In 2012, Williams, now 51, first spoke to PEOPLE about being molested by the 18-year-old daughter of her friend's family while they were away on vacation. She also discussed the incident in her memoir, *You Have No Idea*. 'One night she came into the room where my friend and I were sleeping, and she told me to lie down on the floor. She took my bottoms off and she said, "Be quiet," and she went down on me,' she recounts again on the OWN show. 'I knew it felt good, but also something that was not supposed to be happening.' Williams said she was "conflicted" after it happened and wanted to speak to her family about it. But when she returned home from the trip, she discovered her father's brother passed away, so she chose to suppress the incident. However, she now realizes that despite her best efforts to forget about what happened, it found a way to bubble up to the surface. 'At that young age, having that happen to you in your body, it awakens your sexuality at an age where it shouldn't be awakened,' she said. Williams famously lost her 1983 Miss America crown after racy photos of her in lesbian poses were sold to *Penthouse*. Yet the twice-divorced mother of four went on to have a successful career as a singer and actress, despite never forgetting the incident that had a profound impact on her life. 'I think had that not happened in my life, and I had an opportunity to have a normal courtship with a boyfriend at 16 or whatever ... there wouldn't have been that shame that was always haunting me'" (Dowd, 2014)

According to Recovery Nation (2001-2014):
Common Behaviors Associated with Promiscuity:

- Multiple long-term simultaneous affairs
- Numerous short-term affairs (may or may not be simultaneous)
- Multiple (more than one) sexual partners on a single day
- Multiple (more than five) sexual partners over the course of a single year
- History of multiple sexual encounters with people you've known less than a month
- Indiscriminate sexual encounters with others after getting drunk/high
- Actively searching for sexual encounters when traveling on business
- Establishing "a woman in every port"
- Engaging in prostitution (when the reasons for participating involve anything beyond financial — like a desire for attention/emotional pleasure from pleasing others)
- Hiring of prostitutes/call-girls
- Routine same-sex sexual encounters in public places (e.g. rest rooms, parks)

Elements Frequently Associated with Promiscuity (from the Wheel of Sexual Compulsion):
- Sensory Stimulation (especially physical)
- Accomplishment (when searching for a partner and when engaging in sexual activity)

Other Behaviors Commonly found in a Ritualistic Chain where Promiscuity is the Primary Behavior:
- Danger (especially women getting involved with complete strangers)
- Suspense
- Poly-addiction (especially alcohol/substance abuse)
- Orgasm (more frequent for males than females; especially male-to-male encounters in public settings)
- Fantasy
- Past (especially when sexual abuse/emotional neglect is involved)

Frequent Cues/Triggers Often Associated With Promiscuity
- Alcohol/Substance abuse
- Past history of sexual abuse (especially incestual abuse)
- Past history of emotional neglect (either parental, or long-term partner)
- Low self-esteem
- Emotional imbalance (especially depression, loneliness)

- Opportunity (people, places, times and things)

Boundaries Frequently Violated By Promiscuity:
- Safety (involving STD's, pregnancy, potential violence)
- Honesty
- Self-respect (guilt and shame are often extreme when attempting to engage in sexual behavior with committed partner)
- Intimacy (in all but the rarest occasions, the intimacy that can be experienced with the spouse is sacrificed for the passion and intimacy experienced with the promiscuous partners)
- Family

According to Recovery Nation, "promiscuity may be a way for those with low self-esteem or those with emotional stress to feel needed, desired, useful and wanted by others. Feelings of accomplishment from obtaining multiple sexual partners can be addictive; however, the positive feelings associated with promiscuity are usually short-lived, and feelings of depression, low self-esteem and low worth eventually resurface. Thus, promiscuity becomes a vicious cycle."

The emotional toll from having multiple sexual partners can be very detrimental. Adolescents, in particular, are not mature enough to handle promiscuity, and therefore often end up harming themselves in the long run.

"The impact of these high risk behaviors on one's emotional health includes making dangerous choices that lead to more and more risk. This cycle can lead to problems with self-concept, ineffective relationships, and even depression," Fitzgerald said to Everyday Health.

The main emotional effects of promiscuity seem to be the very symptoms many people are looking to escape through sexual activity. Promiscuous individuals often experience feelings associated with depression, and promiscuity itself can be a symptom of depression. Eventually, for those who are promiscuous due to emotional trauma, feelings of worthlessness and guilt associated with risky sexual behavior always resurface.

"Because of social conditioning and stigmata, pre-marital or extra-marital affairs may foster fear and guilt. Shifting partners often may cause a person to lose confidence in his or her abilities to sustain a healthy relationship, and lower self-esteem," stated Dr Suman Bijlani, a leading gynecologist and obstetrician consulting at the SL Raheja Fortis and Kohinoor Hospitals.

Bijlani indicates not all promiscuous people are suffering emotionally, and changes in cultural norms must be looked at when assessing promiscuity. There is a great drive in the modern world for self-gratification, and for some individuals, having multiple sexual partners is nothing more than a form of pleasurable release (Gillette, 2013)

Most women who lead or have led a promiscuous life suffer many of the debilitating effects listed on the previous pages. As a further consequence, they find it hard to cope in their relationships and with their self-image, even when no one other than themselves is aware of their lifestyle.

If you are one of the many women who suffers silently, it is time for you to take action and establish for yourself a healthy self-esteem by creating a positive self-image.

To rid yourself of the negative feelings that have grown from living a promiscuous life, follow these six steps:

1. **Acknowledge your actions.** Admit them to yourself and to God. Sexual immorality is a sin regardless of the reason one engages in it. Therefore, when you have willfully engaged in an activity that is not pleasing to God, you must repent and turn away from your sin. This may be excruciatingly difficult to do, so allow yourself time to change. After you have established a pattern (negative or positive), it will take some time for you to disengage from the activity/behavior. Be patient with yourself. If you become frustrated with yourself, you may not successfully navigate through the other steps.

2. **Ask God for forgiveness.** Remember to forgive yourself. If you do not forgive yourself, you will not receive God's forgiveness and you will continue to torture yourself about your past acts and choices. You are allowing Satan to have a foothold into your life. Again, be patient with yourself. Although you may ask God for forgiveness with a sincere heart, it

does not automatically mean you will not slip or backslide by repeating old behaviors. The Bible says, "The spirit is willing, but the flesh is weak" (Matthew 26:41 NIV and Mark 14:38 NIV). Your spirit will want to line up with God's word, but the flesh is weak. God will give you strength, for He is your strong tower. Lean on Him. Allow Him to order your steps.

3. **See yourself as valuable.** After engaging in activities that leave you feeling demoralized, unclean, and unworthy, you must rid yourself of that self-image. Learn to see yourself the way God sees you. Psalm 139:14b says, *"I will praise thee; for I am fearfully and wonderfully made: marvellous are thy works; and that my soul knoweth right well."* I Peter 2:9 says, *"But ye are a chosen generation, a royal priesthood, an holy nation, a peculiar people; that ye should shew forth the praises of him who hath called you out of darkness into his marvellous light."* Psalm 8:4-5 tell us, *"What is man, that thou art mindful of him? and the son of man, that thou visitest him? For thou hast made him a little lower than the angels, and hast crowned him with glory and honour."* God created us for greatness. Our past is just that- the past. The past does not dictate

who we are today or the good we can do today. Free your mind from the lies of the evil one, and fill it with the words of God.

4. **Love yourself as you want others to love you.** Rather than looking for love to be emitted from others toward you, allow love to flow from you back to you. The love you show towards yourself must be genuine, just as you want it to be if it were from someone else. Showing love to yourself does not mean buying yourself things or adorning yourself with the finest clothes. To love yourself, you must really like the person you are. Have you ever noticed, the more you like a person, the more you are apt to love her or him? And, the less you like a person, you find it harder to love her or him? Absolutely! Now, that does not negate the agape love of God that we are to have for all mankind as believers. Yes, we strive to love everyone as we are commanded. However, the reality is- if you like a person, you will have an easier time loving her/him. So, get to like yourself. If there are things you do not like about you, change them.

5. **Keep the enemy under your feet,** as you walk through all the steps. The Bible tells us we are not ignorant of Satan's devices (II Corinthians 2:11) and he comes to

steal, kill, and destroy (John 10:10). Your past conditions are not your present conditions. As a believer, you have been washed clean by the blood of Jesus, which was shed on Calvary's cross. And your mindset is different. At one time, you were probably naïvely carefree. You may not have cared who you hurt, and you may not have had the wisdom to know you were hurting yourself. Now that you have come into the knowledge of the truth, begin to make changes.

6. **Delve wholeheartedly into the word of God.** By saturating yourself with the Word, you will keep the enemy at bay. The Word is your covering. It will keep your mind stayed on Him. If you allow the enemy to trick you by telling you, "You do not need the Word," you may easily backslide into your old habits of sexual immorality. Also, you can develop a strong support system with people whom you trust to share your story. They will keep you on the right track, but you must be willing to be honest with them.

Breaking the Chains of
Extended and
Detrimental
Mourning

The Broken Chain
Author unknown

We little knew that morning, that God
Was going to call your name.
In life we loved you dearly,
In death we do the same.
It broke our hearts to lose you,
You did not go alone;
For part of us went with you,
The day God called you home.
You left us peaceful memories,
Your love is still our guide;
And though we cannot see you,
You are always at our side.
Our family chain is broken,
And nothing seems the same;
But as God calls us one by one,
The chain will link again.

A special thanks goes to my aunt Julia Lary who graciously shared this poem with me. This poem was shared with her nearly twenty years ago when her mother (my grandmother) passed from here to glory.

The Bible tells us in the book of Hebrews 9:27, *"It is appointed unto men once to die."* The verse is pretty simple and can be translated as such: Unless we are caught up in the rapture, we will experience physical death to bring our natural life to an end. Physical death is separation of the soul from the body. The body goes back to the earth, and the soul goes back to its creator. Now, even with that truth, death is not always easy to bear, especially when we have lost someone who is near and dear to us. However, in all trials and challenges we encounter, we must always keep at the forefront of our mind that God is in full control and He will be our strength and our comfort.

Because God loves us, He cares about our well-being and our peace of mind. So, to comfort us as we mourn, we have God's word in II Corinthians 5:8 states, *"We are confident, I say, and willing rather to be absent from the body, and to be present with the Lord."* Knowing that our saved loved ones are in the presence of the Lord should be comforting. Also, we can take comfort in knowing God has control over death and He has the final say about when a person's time on earth is up. In Revelation 1:18, Jesus says, *"I am the Living One; I was dead, and now look, I am alive for ever and ever! And I hold the keys of death and Hades."* With this statement, He declares His sovereignty. He holds all power in His hand. I Corinthians 15:55 says, *"O death, where is thy sting? O grave, where is thy victory?"* Death has no control over us. Instead, God controls death. Therefore, we have nothing to fear.

To provide for us greater understanding about death and the time of mourning, the Bible shares numerous accounts of people who have died or have gone through a time of mourning. It would do us well to remember that the word of God is here for our instruction, as well as our reproof.

In Deuteronomy Chapter 34, we have the account of Moses' death, who was a servant of the Lord. Joshua, along with the other Israelites, mourned the death of his leader Moses. They grieved for a period of 30 days. Let us take a closer look into the death of Moses and the resultant time of mourning Joshua endured.

Deuteronomy 34:5-8 says, *"So Moses the servant of the LORD died there in the land of Moab, according to the word of the LORD. And he buried him in a valley in the land of Moab, over against Bethpeor: but no man knoweth of his sepulchre unto this day. And Moses was an hundred and twenty years old when he died: his eye was not dim, nor his natural force abated. And the children of Israel wept for Moses in the plains of Moab thirty days: so the days of weeping and mourning for Moses were ended."* Joshua 1:1-2 says, *"Now after the death of Moses the servant of the LORD it came to pass, that the LORD spake unto Joshua the son of Nun, Moses' minister, saying, 'Moses my servant is dead; now therefore arise, go over this Jordan, thou, and all this people, unto the land which I do give to them, even to the children of Israel.'"*

As a result of Moses' death, Joshua was commanded to continue guiding the Israelites to the Promised Land. In doing so, Joshua was also to divide the land amongst the twelve tribes. In Joshua 1:2, God tells Joshua that his servant Moses is dead, but as Joshua is yet with the living, he has a job to do. Here, we learn that although mourning is permissible, it is to last only for a season. [Is there a certain length of time to mourn? No. Each person will grieve for a different period of time, for each death he/she encounters. And, after the initial period of mourning, one may experience grief occasionally, as he/she continues to live.]

[After we have mourned,] we must continue to go about the Father's business as He has assigned to each of us. Let me remind you of the Great Commission as written in Matthew 28: 18-20,

> *"And Jesus came and spake unto them, saying, 'All power is given unto me in heaven and in earth. Go ye therefore, and teach all nations, baptizing them in the name of the Father, and of the Son, and of the Holy Ghost: Teaching them to observe all things whatsoever I have commanded you: and, lo, I am with you always, even unto the end of the world. Amen.'"*

Joshua was commanded to serve as a guide and a leader for the children of Israel. In Joshua 1:9, Joshua is reminded of his responsibility. It states, *"Have not I commanded thee? Be strong and of a good courage; be not afraid, neither be thou dismayed: for the LORD thy God is with thee whithersoever thou goest."* God also ensures Joshua that He will be with him as he goes. He will be there every step of the way, and He will not forsake him. God tells Joshua to be strong and of good courage. Physically, Joshua is fine; therefore, this statement refers to Joshua's emotional state. God is saying to keep the faith and do not buckle because a loved one has departed from this life. We must believe in who God created us to be.

Those who mentor us will not always be with us; yet, we must persevere In your time(s) of bereavement, remember that mourning is but for a season. We are not to focus on our loss of those who have passed from this life to the point where the grief is overwhelming and detrimental to our livelihood. Like Joshua, we must regroup and focus on our lives that we have left to live. We should ask ourselves the following questions: "When I face the Master will He say, 'Well done, my good and faithful servant'?" "Have I answered the Master's call and been obedient to my calling?" "Have I reached the lost?"

Remember, death is our final act in this life. There is no turning back. But be of good courage; Isaiah 25:8 says that our Lord will swallow up death in victory. That means the saved will live on with Christ. We will see each other again. In this fact, we should rejoice.

(Excerpt from Dr. C. White-Elliott's *Through the Storm* pgs. 144-146)

Now, even after sharing all of that and dissecting one example in God's word, there is much more that needs to be said. So, here we go. Just because something is a part of life and is a natural process, it does not mean that process is easy. Many find death unbearable, and as a result, they find death one of the most difficult occurrences to experience and to overcome. But, I know God does not want us to be immobilized by death. He wants us to experience death in the healthiest possible way. So, I am sure the question that may come to your mind is, "How do we do that?" Keep reading and the answers will unfold.

Before we examine how one can mourn the loss of a loved one without the time of mourning and the loss becoming overwhelming, let us examine the three most difficult types of death to deal with: death of a child, death of a parent, and death of a spouse. Although these three specific categories will be examined, it does not negate the fact there are other deaths people find difficult to endure, such as the death of a close friend, the death of a sibling, and the death of a pet.

Loss of a Child

"Losing a child to death and the grief process related to this loss is generally considered 'one of the most severe, enduring, and debilitating forms of bereavement'" (Oliver, 1999, p. 198) (quoted in Ungureanu & Sandberg, 2010). To assist with the grief that a parent experiences after the loss of a child, "researchers have found religious coping strategies are helpful and seem to be effective especially in situations that 'push people to the bounds of their human limitations' (Pargament et al. 2005, p. 486) (quoted in Ungureanu & Sandberg, 2010).

It has been frequently noted, married couples who experience the death of a child *may* also experience the end of their marriage. This is namely due to the differences in the grieving processes of husbands and wives. The research that has been done on this subject yielded the following consensus: Wives tend "to be more expressive with their grief (i.e., more willing to talk about the child and his/her death, more crying, more need of closeness for comfort), while the husbands tend to be more withdrawn and feel a need to be more in control of their emotional reactions by intellectualizing their pain" (Ungureanu & Sandberg, 2010, p. 307).

The research further revealed, husbands "expressed a need to be strong for their wives, who seemed to be overwhelmed with grief" (Ungureanu & Sandberg, 2010, p. 307). When husbands and wives respond differently, "husbands may in turn grow angry and frustrated with their wives' grieving process and then become unable to offer comfort to their wives. Wives then become angry at their husbands' withdrawal and supposed unwillingness to share in the pain (Ungureanu & Sandberg)." Men and women must understand God designed them differently and just because one responds to the child's death in one particular manner, which may be different from the other's method of mourning, it does not mean that parent loves the child any less or is mourning for the child any less. Husbands and wives must give each other the space to grieve in their own way and refrain from being judgmental based upon what is shown on the outer appearance.

To assist parents in dealing with their loss and solidifying their marriage during such a trying time, couples can seek social support "in support groups, reaching out to friends and family, and involvement in receiving help from church congregations" (Ungureanu & Sandberg, 2010, p. 308). "Religious coping strategies may be useful in unique ways. Not only may individuals find meaning in their experience, but they also may reach out to God, clergy, or other members of their church community. It seems that through a collaborative style of coping, parents can find comfort in their God when carrying the burden of mourning a child in a unique way" (p. 313).

All in all, when a parent mourns the loss of a child, he or she may mourn in a way that is unique to any other parent who has suffered the same loss. There is not one perfect technique that can be offered to a parent that will make the mourning process less unbearable. The parent has to go through the process at his/her own pace and find a peaceful state in which he/she can move forward. Read the true testimony below of a woman I will call Stephanie.

In 1978, Stephanie gave birth to her first child, a son Michael, who would eventually be an older brother to Stephanie's other three children, who would be born later. After Michael turned seventeen, he was diagnosed with HIV. At age thirty, Michael's HIV developed into full-blown AIDS. Three years later, Michael succumbed to the illness and departed this life, leaving Stephanie and her two daughters and second son to mourn.

When I interviewed Stephanie, she shared it took four years to really get to a point of healing after the loss of her son. Also, she revealed she continues to mourn as other events occur and cause her to remember and miss the presence of her son. What gave Stephanie solace in the passing of her son was knowing he had accepted the Lord Jesus Christ as his personal savior. What she cared most about was his eternal resting place. Knowing he is in the bosom of the Lord gives her some peace, but of course, she still longs for his presence, his conversation, his love, and precious moments.

As Stephanie continues to live on this side of eternity, I pray for her continued peace and comfort as she yet mourns the absence of her son. A child is irreplaceable and a parent's grief should never be minimalized or brushed aside. Parents never expect to give life to a child, see the child come into the world, teach child the essentials of life, and then have to bury the child. That is not the natural cycle of life. However, the unexpected, the unanticipated, and the unplanned may happen, and there is no way to prepare for it emotionally. Sometimes, however, the child suffers from an illness and the parents realize death is imminent. And even then, the reality is yet hard to cope with.

So parents, allow yourselves time to grieve. But in your grief, do not neglect your own health or the livelihood of other children you may have. Remember, even in death there is yet life. When one person dies, there are others who are yet alive and count on you. As much as you can, be there for them, and allow them to be there for you. Together, there is strength!

Loss of a Parent

Saying goodbye to a parent is one of the hardest things we face in our lives. When a parent dies, whether through old age, unexpectedly, or from disease, children [of all ages] are left with a range of emotions ranging from emptiness and loneliness to guilt and anger. The most common emotions and normal reactions include:

- Confusion
- Anxiety

- Remorse
- Fear
- Frustration
- Yearning
- Depression (All Psychology Centers, 2013).

As with all grieving, special occurrences such as birthdays and holidays are especially difficult when surviving the loss of a parent. Renewed grief on these occasions is known as an anniversary reaction, and while these reactions can re-occur for years, they are most common for the first three to 24 months. These types of anniversary reactions are even more pronounced in [adolescent] children.

According to psychologist J. W. Worden, and the Harvard Child Bereavement Study (HCBS), [adolescent] children have four "tasks" of mourning they must accomplish in order to process the death of a parent:

- They must accept the reality of the parent's death.
- They must experience the grieving and emotional pain of the loss.
- They must adjust to the world in which the deceased is no longer there.
- They must find ways to memorialize the deceased, and relocate the lost parent within his or her life in a different way.

Behavioral grief symptoms in [adolescent] children include:

- Withdrawal
- Searching for the deceased
- Avoiding places and people who remind them of the deceased

- Changes in eating habits
- Crying

Adolescent grief is an area of continuing interest and research. Teenagers experience such a varying and dynamic range of emotions, sometimes responding to psychological tests as adults, sometimes through avoidance or masking of emotions, and sometimes they respond as children. However, we do know that adolescents are susceptible to short and long-term emotional damage from the loss of a parent. Teenagers may act out through risk-taking behavior, and disinterest in school and activities is common following the loss of a parent.

Read the following account of a now thirty-year-old woman who suffered the loss of both her parents when she was sixteen years old and how she learned to cope while she is yet dealing with her loss. The following account is her recollection of the details of the two traumatic and life-changing events.

In 2001, at sixteen years of age, Octavia was the fourth child of her father with two younger siblings after her. On Feb. 19, 2001, Drena, Octavia's mother, gave birth to her sixth child, giving Octavia another younger brother. Just hours after giving birth, Drena was placed on life support, after having suffered problems with her breathing for months. The breathing problems were exacerbated by the delivery, and her breathing eventually failed. Octavia's immediate reaction to her mother's condition was one of shock. However, she believed her mother would pull through. Nevertheless, the reality was Drena would succumb to the affliction her body was suffering.

Three days later, two of Octavia's older siblings made the choice to remove Drena from life support. All family members were asked to be present, if they so desired. Octavia opted not to be present to see her mother take her last breath. After Drena's soul was commended back to the Lord Jesus Christ, Octavia experienced a range of emotions.

First, she felt confused, lost, and full of regret. She thought and asked of God, "Can't you bring her back? I want to say goodbye." Notice this, at sixteen, Octavia realized her mother's time was up here on earth, even though she was leaving behind a newborn baby, two adolescents, and two teenagers. Drena's oldest son was twenty-one at the time of her passing. Octavia did not request her mother's return to be permanent. She just wanted enough time to say goodbye. She desired proper closure. However, death does not always provide that opportunity. Most people are required to obtain closure after the other person has departed this life.

Second, Octavia was deeply concerned about her two younger siblings. Because Octavia and her siblings were already in the care of their father years prior to their mother's passing, Octavia along with her father and older brother were primary caregivers for the younger ones. During that time, Octavia drew her two younger brothers in much closer. When the newborn left the hospital, prior to Drena being taken off life support, he was immediately taken into the care of Octavia's older brother.

Third, Octavia needed to build a support system that would comfort and console her. Thankfully, Octavia already had that in place. She and her siblings comforted one another. Her father was there to console her. Her church family and natural family were there to console her.

As Octavia was learning to cope with life without her mother and attend to the physical and emotional needs of her three younger brothers, five months later, she was faced with the equally sudden passing of her father.

One day, Octavia's father Antonio, Sr. dropped Octavia off at her grandmother's home. The plan was for Octavia to spend the night. That night, as Octavia and her grandmother attempted to sleep, neither could. When morning came, Octavia walked into the kitchen and overheard her grandmother and other family members discussing a car accident. Octavia immediately thought of her two younger brothers and became frantic. She thought they were in the car. Thankfully, they were not. Sorrowfully, Octavia's father passed that morning in the car accident.

The next week, when it was time for the home going service, Octavia had no desire to attend her father's service. She just could not say goodbye. However, her older sister told her she needed to go. Octavia consented.

With her father's death, Octavia suffered great grief because she felt she had lost her security blanket. Inwardly, she asked, "Who is going to take care of me? Who is going to protect me?" The death of Antonio, Sr. was much harder for Octavia to bear because as her father, he was her protector and her caregiver.

Losing both parents in the span of five months, unexpectedly, and at a young age was extremely difficult for Octavia. Her coping mechanisms were and still are her relationship with God, prayer, and taking time to process her thoughts when she is alone. Year by year, the losses have become more bearable. However, there are specific occasions and times during the year when Octavia feels the loss of her parents more than at other times. These times have included and may still include Mother and Father's Day, birthdays, the anniversary of their deaths, and the birth of Octavia's own three children (especially the first one).

In order to successfully work through the grief of a parent's death, individuals need to be completely open to dealing with their emotions, to express them honestly, and discuss them with someone who can provide support. Only through this process will a person be able to resolve his or her grief.

(All information on dealing with the loss of a parent is credited to the All Psychology Careers Organization via its website from the article titled "Loss of a Parent.")

Loss of a Spouse

According to Jim Ewens, a chaplain and co-director of a Milwaukee hospice, "There is no more painful time in life than surviving the death of a spouse or close loved one" (quoted in Bauer, 1996). As a person endures the pain of the loss of his/her spouse, getting support from others may be difficult. From Ewens' experience, "as a society, we're uncomfortable with [a grieving person's] tears. But a person in grief is in a delicate state and can't be pushed. Grieving takes time" (quoted in Bauer).

As a co-director of a hospice facility, Ewens has witnessed many people say goodbye to their spouses and other loved ones. While serving as a chaplain at the same facility, Ewens has counseled many bereaved persons, according to Bauer's

(1996) article, and he and Bauer collectively drew the following conclusions,

Spending a weekend in a group can help people in mourning. It gives them a safe place to talk about how they feel with others who understand. Usually it takes about a year to accept the death, realize there is a future worth living for, and move on alone. Even then, memories or events such as an anniversary often trigger a resurgence of grief. But if the death is sudden, such as from a heart attack or accident, the loss will be much tougher to handle. Survivors are bombarded with emotions: sadness, anger, guilt, self-reproach, loneliness, yearning, helplessness and fatigue. Those in mourning really struggle psychically. Friends and family should encourage the spouse to talk about the person who has died. With support, people can weather great difficulty, but others become stuck in their anger or grieve past the time when they should move on. The tough part is knowing how to be supportive without pushing the grieving person too far. The risk is that the person will take the grief underground, which could lead to serious depression (Bauer, 1996).

To get a personalized account from someone who actually experienced the death of a spouse, I interviewed Priscilla Darwin. Here is Priscilla's story:

In 2007, after having been married for 30 years, Priscilla lost her husband to inoperable cancer of the aorta, which spread to his lungs. Many times, when a loved one is diagnosed with a terminal illness, the family has time to prepare mentally, physically, emotionally, and financially for the loved one's death. However, in Priscilla's case, her husband was diagnosed in March 2007, and in December of the same year, he passed. To say the least, Priscilla's life was turned asunder. She had to learn how to be alone. She could no longer share meals with her husband, visit him in the yard as he worked, or place her arms around him as he slept. Instead, she had one major void to attend to. After his death, she found herself alone. Priscilla and her husband had raised two children who were adults at the time of their father's passing. Priscilla and her two children grieved separately, not together as a family. That was yet another disconcerting element in Priscilla's life.

Priscilla's mourning period lasted three to four years. At the time of her husband's passing, Priscilla was unable to grieve immediately because there was much to do to prepare for his burial and to maintain the regular occurrences in her life, such as, paying and maintaining household bills. When Priscilla did slow down enough to allow herself a proper period of grief, she found she was truly alone. The people who were close to her did not truly understand her loss, not having been there themselves. She had no one to talk to, and when she saw other couples in public, her heart sank. To try and find solace and some semblance of healing, Priscilla sought out therapy in the form of group sessions. She desired to be with others who knew what she was going through. One institution referred her to a group session. Priscilla attended the session, but left feeling worse than she had when she entered. As a believer, Priscilla operates according to her faith in God. The other group members, who participated in the session, were not believers and, therefore, responded to the death of their spouses in carnal manners, such as with anger and blaming or questioning God.

Looking back on her experience with losing her husband of thirty years, Priscilla offers the following advice: first, families should mourn together in order to draw closer together and to bear one another's pain, and second, the grieving spouse should find a support group made up of persons who are dealing with the same loss and have the same spiritual walk.

II Corinthians 6:14, says, "Do not be yoked together with unbelievers. For what do righteousness and wickedness have in common? Or what fellowship can light have with darkness?" Although this verse is specifically referring to idol worship, it can be applied to others avenues of life. We, as believers, should be careful about the prolonged company we keep with unbelievers. Unhealthy habits of others can rub off on us.

In Priscilla's case, as a believer, she desired to be healed with use of God's word and through carnal advents. Thus, it would have been better for her to align herself with spiritually minded people.

Whether one has experienced the loss of a child, a parent, a spouse, a friend, or a sibling, it is imperative to the psychological, emotional, and physical health of the bereaved to mourn in a manner that will allow him/her to positively come to terms with the loved one's death.

Five Stages of Mourning

According to Julie Axelrod (2006), "The stages of mourning and grief are universal and are experienced by people from all walks of life. There are five stages of normal grief that were first proposed by Elisabeth Kübler-Ross in her 1969 book *On Death and Dying*." As quoted in Axelrod, Kubler-Ross says, "In our bereavement, we spend different lengths of time working through each step and express each stage with different levels of intensity. The five stages do not necessarily occur in any specific order."

All people grieve differently. Some people will wear their emotions on their sleeve and be outwardly emotional. Others will experience their grief more internally, and may not cry. You should try and not judge *how* a person experiences their grief, as each person will experience it differently."

1. *Denial and Isolation-* a normal first reaction to the death of a loved one is to experience denial and isolation, denying the reality of the death. "It is a defense mechanism that buffers the immediate shock."

2. *Anger-* "As the masking effects of denial and isolation begin to wear, reality and its pain re-emerge. The anger may be aimed at inanimate objects, complete strangers, friends or family. Anger may be directed at our dying or deceased loved one. Rationally, we know the person is not to be blamed. Emotionally, however, we may resent the person for causing us

pain or for leaving us. We feel guilty for being angry, and this makes us angrier."

3. *Bargaining-* "The normal reaction to feelings of helplessness and vulnerability is often a need to regain control." So, we rationalize how we could have prevented the person's death or how we could have treated him/her better. Instead of making us feel better, these thoughts make us feel worse and can lead us into stage four.

4. *Depression-* "Two types of depression are associated with mourning. The first one is a reaction to practical implications relating to the loss. Sadness and regret predominate this type of depression. We worry about the costs and burial. The second type of depression is more subtle and, in a sense, perhaps more private. It is our quiet preparation to separate and to bid our loved one farewell."

5. *Acceptance-* "Reaching this stage of mourning is a gift not afforded to everyone. Death may be sudden and unexpected or we may never see beyond our anger or denial. This phase is marked by withdrawal and calm. This is not a period of happiness and must be distinguished from depression. Coping with loss is an ultimately a deeply personal and singular experience — nobody can help you go through it more easily or understand all the emotions that you're going through. But others can be there for you and help comfort you through this process. The best thing you can do is to allow yourself to feel the grief as it comes over you. Resisting it only will prolong the natural process of healing" (quoted in Axelrod, 2006).

There are some general guidelines, however, that will allow you to mend more quickly and completely:

1. Remember that no matter how much pain you may feel, you will survive your loss.
2. Emotional ups and downs are a normal part of any grieving process. Here's the paradox: In order to get past the difficult feelings, you must experience them.
3. Don't try to speed up or avoid the process. If you do, you will not heal properly. Your grieving will have been incomplete, and your energy to deal with the present will remain bound to the past.
4. Care for yourself as if you are caring for a dear friend. Rest, eat well (even if you aren't hungry), and exercise (even if you don't want to). Avoid other changes and don't make big decisions unless you absolutely must.
5. Ask those you love and trust for support. You don't have to face this alone.
6. Write about your loss. Journaling will bring your unexpressed emotions to the surface, thereby encouraging the grieving process to move along.
7. Create your own ritual. Most cultures have ceremonies to mark death. A ritual marking any loss helps us to acknowledge that the loss is real. It is a way to honor the loss, and to separate the past from the present. When faced with any kind of

a loss, feel free to create any kind of ceremony that holds meaning for you." (From "The Truth about Grief and Loss" by Maud Purcell, LCSW, CEAP)

The word of God is our comfort. Below is a list of scriptures you can read during your bereavement period.

Scriptures on Death

1 Thessalonians 4:13-14

"But I would not have you to be ignorant, brethren, concerning them which are asleep, that ye sorrow not, even as others which have no hope. For if we believe that Jesus died and rose again, even so them also which sleep in Jesus will God bring with him."

2 Thessalonians 2:16-17

"Now our Lord Jesus Christ himself, and God, even our Father, which hath loved us, and hath given us everlasting consolation and good hope through grace, Comfort your hearts, and establish you in every good word and work."

Matthew 5:4

"Blessed are they that mourn: for they shall be comforted."

2 Corinthians 1:3-4

"Blessed be God, even the Father of our Lord Jesus Christ, the Father of mercies, and the God of all comfort; Who comforteth us in all our tribulation, that we may be able to comfort them which are in any trouble, by the comfort wherewith we ourselves are comforted of God."

2 Corinthians 5:8

"We are confident, I say, and willing rather to be absent from the body, and to be present with the Lord."

Psalms 119:50

"This is my comfort in my affliction: for thy word hath quickened me."

Psalm 23

"Yea, though I walk through the valley of the shadow of death, I will fear no evil: for thou art with me; thy rod and thy staff they comfort me."

Isaiah 49:13b

"for the Lord hath comforted his people, and will have mercy upon his afflicted."

Isaiah 61:1-3

"The Spirit of the Lord God is upon me; because the Lord hath anointed me to preach good tidings unto the meek; he hath sent me to bind up the brokenhearted, to proclaim liberty to the captives, and the opening of the prison to them that are bound; To proclaim the acceptable year of the Lord, and the day of vengeance of our God; to comfort all that mourn; To appoint unto them that mourn in Zion, to give unto them beauty for ashes, the oil of joy for mourning, the garment of praise for the spirit of heaviness; that they might be called trees of righteousness, the planting of the Lord, that he might be glorified."

Isaiah 41:10

"Fear thou not; for I am with thee: be not dismayed; for I am thy God: I will strengthen thee; yea, I will help thee; yea, I will uphold thee with the

*right hand of my
righteousness."*

Isaiah 51:11

*"Therefore the redeemed of
the Lord shall return, and
come with singing unto Zion;
and everlasting joy shall be
upon their head: they shall
obtain gladness and joy; and
sorrow and mourning shall
flee away."*

1 Peter 5:7

*"Casting all your care upon
him; for he careth for you."*

1 Corinthians 15:55-57

*"O death, where is thy sting?
O grave, where is thy victory?
The sting of death is sin; and
the strength of sin is the law.
But thanks be to God, which
giveth us the victory through
our Lord Jesus Christ."*

Revelations 21:4

*"And God shall wipe away all
tears from their eyes; and
there shall be no more death,
neither sorrow, nor crying,
neither shall there be any
more pain: for the former
things are passed away."*

Breaking the Chains of
the effects of
Broken
Relationships

Of all the various types of calamity that befall us during our lifetime, a broken relationship is a calamity that can be expurgated from our life if we are willing. A relationship does not remain broken unless both parties are not willing to mend it. Throughout our lifetime, we develop relationships with our family members, friends, spouses, coworkers, neighbors, church members, schoolmates, etc. Some relationships are for but a season while others can last nearly a lifetime. Some relationships carry on with not so much as a bump in the road while others suffer through knockdown drag out fights. Some relationships can endure any storm while others are broken and damaged. Broken relationships can cause one to endure great heartache, great emotional distress and many sleepless nights.

In this chapter, we will explore and discuss how a relationship can become broken and what it may take for the relationships to be mended. In our exploration, we will examine three types of relationships that can suffer brokenness but can be healed and restored: parent/child relationship, love relationships, and friendships.

As you read this chapter, keep in mind these words from II Corinthians 5:18: *"And all things are of God, who hath reconciled us to himself by Jesus Christ, and hath given to us the ministry of reconciliation."* God reconciled mankind back to Himself through the death and shed blood of His son Jesus. Now, we can use the same ministry of reconciliation to reconcile others to Christ and to us. The tools are already here. We just need to use them. As you read this chapter, the tools will be revealed unto you.

Parent/Child Relationships

Parent-child relationships can suffer brokenness as a result of divorce, miscommunication, and/or a lack of parental involvement. When parents divorce, both the father and mother must ensure constant contact with the children, particularly the noncustodial parent. When parents divorce, one parent normally shifts from seeing the children daily to seeing them on the weekends or every other weekend only. The lack of parental involvement in a child's life can be very damaging, especially if the child has a strong bond with the parent. If the bond does not continue to be strengthened and becomes weakened or severed, the child may fail to develop a bond with that parent's family members as well, unless an adult family member steps in and establishes his/her own relationship with the child.

Evelyn Smith shared her story by way of an article of how a broken relationship with her father caused her relationship and interaction with his family to be severed. It is paraphrased below.

When Evelyn was seven years old, her parents divorced. Due to the divorce, Evelyn did not interact with her father or his family. From her recollection, the little interaction she did encounter with her father's family was very negative and therefore disconcerting. Because of the negative interactions, Evelyn soon developed a hardened heart towards her father's family. However, she did not fully understand her disdain towards them until she had to address the issue head on.

Years later, as a married adult, Evelyn was contacted by her first cousin Joyce whom she had never met. Joyce was in the process of completing the genealogy of their family and thought it would be helpful to acquire Evelyn's assistance. When Joyce contacted Evelyn, Evelyn informed Joyce she did not know the family's history due to the severed relationship with her father that she suffered as a child. It was at that moment Evelyn realized the range of emotions she was still harboring from her childhood. Despite Joyce's failed attempt to obtain information from her cousin, she continued to email Evelyn.

As a child, Evelyn had actually met Joyce's parents, and they had been kind and considerate towards her. When Evelyn experienced the same sweetness and kindness in Joyce, Evelyn gladly responded to Joyce's emails that sometimes came daily. As part of Joyce's inquiry regarding the family, she inquired about the family plot that is located at a cemetery not far from Evelyn's home. Evelyn express to Joyce she had not been there since she was seven years old. However, one day Evelyn and her husband decided to visit the cemetery and obtain Joyce's requested information. At the cemetery, Evelyn found the family plot overgrown with weeds and thickets. The visual she received of the burial plot quickly reminded her of her heart condition toward her father's family. She knew through that incident God was talking to her about her emotional condition.

After that experience, she quickly wanted to clean up her emotional condition as well at the family plot. At the gravesite she saw the grave of her younger brother who had died at birth when she was seven years old along with the gravesite of her grandfather. So many memories of heartache came flooding back. Evelyn believed if she physically cleaned the plot, it would allow God to spiritually clean her broken emotional condition.

As time went on, Joyce and Evelyn together cleaned the family plot. Through their interaction they became close, and Evelyn was delivered from the pain and suffering she had experienced from her childhood trauma. As a demonstration of her healing, she quotes Psalm 147:3: "He heals the brokenhearted and binds up their wounds."

When Evelyn discovered the disdain and brokenness she carried around, she immediately sought out a solution to rid herself of the ill feelings. She had a desired to be whole and found her healing and deliverance from the past in her present relationship with God. She moved herself out of the way, and she did not make excuses about why she had a right to feel the way she did. She sought healing from the Great I Am. He is the God who heals us through His healing virtue. Evelyn serves as an example for so many of us who walk around with hurts and disappointments. We must understand hurts and disappointments are debilitating to our emotional and sometimes physical well-being. Undue stress can cause ulcers, cancers, etc. Be free today, in the name of Jesus.

Another account of a broken relationship between a parent and child follows. This account is my personal testimony.

During my childhood, I suffered a momentary broken relationship with my mother due to a lack of communication and misguided thinking. To clarify, it was my lack of communication and my misguided/immature thinking, not hers.

After experiencing sexual abuse from close family members throughout my adolescent years, when I became a teenager, I began to separate myself from my mother. It took me another fifteen years to fully understand why I behaved in such a manner. At the age of twenty-eight, I began to revisit my experiences and my blatant attitude toward my loving mother. To put it quite frankly, she did not deserve my negative attitude towards her, for she loved me and cared for me deeply.

At twenty-eight, as I looked back over my life, I realized I blamed my mother for everything I had experienced even though she had no knowledge of what I had to endure. As a child and as a teenager, I believed as my sole parent, she was my provider and my protector. I also believed she should have been aware of what was happening to me and that she should have not been so trusting. As an adolescent, I truly believed she failed to protect me. That belief caused me to retreat from her and harbor emotions of dislike.

However, at nearly thirty years of age, I realized there was no way she could have protected me from something she did not realize was occurring. As a young mother, she did the best she could with her limited knowledge.

When I had my epiphany about the reality of our situation, I quickly mended my relationship with my mother by sharing with her all I had endured. Because she had no prior knowledge of the abuse I had suffered, she quickly became to understand why a wedge had been forced between her and her only daughter. From that point forward, my mother and I walked hand-in-hand and heart-to-heart as we had done before my teenage years. I learned through trial and error that effective communication is the key to building a healthy relationship between any two individuals.

My recommendation to any child who harbors feeling against his or her parents is to open up and share with the parents what those feelings are and how they came to be, to the best of one's ability. Do not wait until tomorrow. Do it today! Tomorrow is not promised to anyone, and you do not want to live a life of regrets. My mother departed this life four years ago, but I had the opportunity to share with her my feelings and thoughts nearly fourteen years before her death. I had an opportunity to mend the broken fence, and I seized it. Was it easy? No! I did not ever want to tell my mother what had occurred in my past. But, at the same time, it was more important to me to have a healthy relationship with her at the present and to give her an understanding of why I behaved the way I had toward her.

It is my recommendation that if your parent is still alive today, take the opportunity to mend a broken fence, and do not let another moment pass you!

Love (Eros) Relationships

Read the following article "What God Teaches Us About Broken Marriage Vows" by Bronwyn Lea. It discusses the entanglements of divorce and God's perspective as demonstrated in His word.

Many divorced Christians have felt they step into church wearing a scarlet D. Author Elisabeth Corcoran was one of these. After her marriage of almost 19 years unraveled, Corcoran grappled with pain, confusion, and shame. Those feelings were compounded when she was politely asked to step down from speaking at a church women's Christmas event soon after her divorce. Hush-hush, of course.

Following the recent release of her book, Unraveling: The End of a Christian Marriage, *she moderates an online Facebook group for divorcees. She has heard hundreds of similar stories. Divorcees often hear the words "God hates divorce" from others. "I know," one woman wrote. "I'm not such a fan myself."*

While research shows that marriages between actively practicing believers fare significantly better than others, the divorce rate within the church is still alarmingly high. Sadly, rather than experiencing the church as a place of comfort and restoration, divorcees often face a guilt-tripping response.

Differences in interpretation about when the Bible allows divorce (if ever) leaves some Christians feeling our hands are tied when we long to extend them in compassion. Plus, our deeply held belief that "it takes two" to make a marriage work mistakenly translates into a belief that "it takes two" to break a marriage up. We subconsciously assign blame accordingly.

However, the truth is that it only takes one to wreck a covenant, as we can learn from God's own relationship with the northern kingdom of Israel.

Our own understanding of marriage is modeled on the very covenant God made with his people. As David Instone-Brewer explains in Divorce and Remarriage in the Church, *God was Israel's husband (Isa. 54:5), who took her to be his own and vowed to feed, clothe, cherish, and be faithful to her. In stark contrast to God's faithfulness and care, Israel and Judah shamelessly disregarded the covenant: neglecting, abusing and betraying him. The prophets repeatedly called their behavior out as the violation of the covenant it was: adultery (Ezek. 23:37, Jer. 5:7).*

God's marital covenant with the northern kingdom of Israel had been wrecked by her hardhearted behavior, and in Jeremiah 3:8 we hear these words: "for all the adulteries of that faithless one, Israel, I had sent her away with a decree of divorce." In Isaiah 50:1, he asks, "Where is your mother's certificate of divorce, with which I sent her away?"

God warns adulterous and apostate Judah to learn a lesson from Israel's example. Both sister states had been unfaithful and broken their covenants with God, but while God had divorced Israel, he offered Judah a second (and third, and fourth) chance at mercy. His offer of restoration was beautifully enacted by Hosea in his marriage to unfaithful Gomer, and ultimately realized in the unbreakable marriage covenant between Christ and the church.

I had often noted God's patient forgiveness and covenant renewal in Hosea, but God's description of his own divorce with the northern kingdom of Israel shocked me. I had unquestioningly internalized the phrase "the sin of divorce." Regardless of how I interpreted the debate about Jesus' words on the topic, if God himself had experienced this unfaithfulness, I needed to rethink my understanding of sin and divorce.

Let me be clear: Marriage covenants are meant to be permanent, and sin is always to blame when a marriage ends in divorce. We commit sin when we break our vows, and marriage requires the regular practice of confession and forgiveness for the failures and oversights between spouses. There is a difference, though, between minor, unintentional mistakes and willful violations of covenant vows. In the former, we are to forgive and "bear with one another in love." In the latter, God allowed the victim a choice: to remain and forgive as he did with Judah, or to divorce where a covenant has been broken by "hardness of heart," as happened with Israel.

The sin in divorce lies in the breaking of marriage vows, not necessarily in the divorce itself. God's own divorce was entirely due to Israel's hardhearted sin. God was the blameless victim of divorce. When God says "I hate divorce" (Mal. 2:16), he says so not with the furious pointed finger of a judge, but with the broken-heartedness of One who has experienced the devastation of rejection and betrayal at the hands of his beloved.

Divorce is not God's will or desire for us. Even where divorce is allowed, it is not commanded, and then it is still a tragedy. Divorce leaves behind devastation and victims in its wake.

That God himself is a divorcee, despite his faultless covenant faithfulness, calls us to a more nuanced understanding of marriage and divorce. In our own marriages, God calls us to follow his example of covenant faithfulness, and has demonstrated how much grace and forgiveness is needed to maintain a relationship in the face of human sinfulness. God's example gives us a framework to talk meaningfully about commitment and grace, and yet also to say that in situations of hard-hearted and deliberate covenant violation, divorce was allowed as God's way of officially declaring a broken covenant "broken."

We find wisdom when we view hot topics within the larger framework of Scripture. A discussion on purity should not just be about whether a person is a virgin when they marry (even if they've done "everything but"), but about how they steward their sexuality throughout their lives. Similarly, the litmus test for covenant faithfulness in marriage should not just be about whether or not someone got divorced (even if they did "everything but"), but about how we steward our marriages and make daily attempts to model God's faithfulness to our spouses.

God calls us to covenant faithfulness. We need to mourn the sins we commit when we fail to keep our vows to our spouses before we lament the "sin of divorce." Upholding and honoring marriage is not going to be accomplished by shaming and opposing divorce as much as it is by our gracious and firm commitment to upholding wedding-day vows of love, nurture, care, and faithfulness. We are called to consider covenant faithfulness long before we consider divorce, and we are called to grace in the tragic event that divorce does happen.

As stated in the article, divorce is a choice. If couples find their relationship headed towards divorce, there are steps they can take to get their marriage back on track, if they so desire. Those steps will be discussed in great detail at the end of the chapter.

Friendships (Platonic) Relationships

As individuals, we learn much about life and relationships from observation but more so from experience. Elizabeth Bernstein shares in the article "Delicate Art of Fixing a Broken Friendship" her personal experiences of how platonic friendships can go awry and what steps can be taken to mend them if they should become damaged. Read her article below:

A friend emailed me one evening to say she felt I wasn't there when she needed me.
I was stunned. I reminded her that I'd already spoken with her twice that day about a problem she had. She

replied with a list of all the things she ever did for me. We bickered, via email, for the better part of an hour. Then angry and hurt, I typed these words and hit 'send': "This friendship isn't working for me anymore. I am bowing out."

Whoa... How was I going to fix that?

Some friendships are meant to end. Pals move away, grow apart, or something happens to make it clear that the relationship isn't mutually beneficial anymore. The memories are good, but it's time to move on.

Last year, I wrote about how to terminate a friendship efficiently and kindly, minimizing collateral damage with mutual friends and leaving the door open for possible future reconciliation ("How to Break Up with a Friend").

Because here's the thing with friendship breakups: Sometimes you come to regret them.

Make-Up Kit

Here are some tips for mending a broken friendship.

- *When in doubt, err on the side of trying to reconcile.*
- *Vent to a third party who is supportive of the friendship, not to your estranged friend.*
- *You may be ready to make up, but don't assume your friend is, too. Invite your friend to work with you.*
- *Ask what you did wrong—and listen to the answer. Apologize. Take it slow. Rebuilding trust takes time.*

A good friend is an emotional safe haven, providing support, guidance and laughter. When someone like that is suddenly gone from your life, it can be heart-wrenching. But how do you go about rebuilding a friendship that has splintered? When do you reach out? What do you say, and what if your former friend doesn't want to hear it? Texting "I'm sorry" probably won't cut it.

It bears saying that it's best not to let conflict become a crisis in the first place. "A relationship is an active process, and a repair should be an ongoing process, as well," says Frederic Luskin, a psychologist, director of the Forgiveness Project at Stanford University, which researches how forgiveness is good for mental and physical health, and author of "Forgive for Good."

"You need to pay attention and not just be wrapped up in what you need to say," he says. If you have an argument, address the situation right away. Acknowledge your friend's feelings. Ask him to tell you how he feels. Apologize.

If you do end up estranged from your friend, find a way to make peace—even if you feel you weren't at fault or the forgiving isn't mutual. Forgiveness—asking for it and granting it—is good for your health. Research shows it lowers your blood pressure, decreases depression and has a positive effect on the nervous system, says Dr. Luskin.

Is there a time limit on mending a broken friendship? It depends, the experts say. Time can make the situation worse, allowing people to stew in their grievances too long, or letting them forget what was good about the union in the first place. But often time heals—especially if the parties mellow, mature or otherwise change their perspectives.

"What is important is what happens during the time of non-communication," says Daniel L. Shapiro, a psychologist, director of the Harvard International Negotiation Program and co-author of "Beyond Reason: Using Emotions as You Negotiate." "Am I trying to better understand myself and my estranged friend's perspective?" he asks. "Or am I demonizing the other?"

Dr. Shapiro works with negotiators who are political adversaries or from estranged countries, to help them cope with the emotional dimension of conflict and negotiation and to deal more effectively with their differences. He teaches each side to dig beneath complicated emotions that may bog down the reconciliation process, and focus on five core concerns to foster positive feelings: Appreciation—meaning each party needs to feel heard and valued. Autonomy—each side needs freedom to decide if and when he or she wants to make up. Affiliation—each side needs to close the distance to regain closeness. Status—each needs to recognize that they contributed to the conflict. Role—each needs to adopt the position of listener, problem solver or healer.

Each side needs to be patient. Friends trying to reconcile shouldn't expect an immediate return to closeness, Dr. Shapiro says. They need to regain trust.

At first, I was reluctant to make up with my friend. I was hurt that she'd lashed into me. She responded to my silence over the next few days by periodically emailing me goofy photos of cute animals, which only irritated me more. I told her I needed space; she told me to take as long as I needed, that she would be patient.

Then my mom piped up. She knew how much this friendship meant to me. After hearing my side of the argument, she told me to stop being so stubborn and apologize. So I wrote my pal and said, "I miss you and I'm sorry I'm such an idiot." She excitedly responded that she was sorry too and happy to move on. (It pains me to admit that no matter how old I get, mom often still knows best.)

A few years ago, Wendy Knight, 46, a publicist in Panton, Vt., accused a very good friend of hers of hitting on her boyfriend. The friend was speechless and said she would never do that. The next day, the woman told Ms. Knight in an email that there was no point in being friends if she really felt that way. "I was actually surprised," Ms. Knight recalls. "I thought, 'Wait a minute, I didn't think this is how she would respond.' How silly of me."

Over the next year, Ms. Knight realized she was devastated over the loss of her friend. The two had often hiked and shared meals together. They had supported each other through relationship breakups and the loss of two parents. Now that Ms. Knight had broken up with her boyfriend, she missed her girlfriend.

So Ms. Knight composed a handwritten letter of apology to her friend saying she regretted causing her so much pain. She explained that she had taken the insecurity she felt in her relationship with her boyfriend out on her friend, and asked for her forgiveness. She told her friend how much she missed her.

The friend called immediately. She said that she cried when she read the letter. The two women chatted and slowly began renewing a friendship, emailing and talking on the phone regularly. Ms. Knight went to visit her friend in Texas, where she'd moved. Then they started going on vacations together. Today they are closer than ever.

As a friend, you must make the choice whether or not a friendship has run its course or if it is worth salvaging. Platonic relationships, just as other relationships, have their ups and their downs. We must work hard to maintain them, if we value them. Using the steps listed above as well as those shared below can help you to restore broken friendships.

Salvaging and/or Restoring Broken Relationships

Now that we have surveyed several examples of broken parent/child relationships, love relationships, and friend-ships, let us examine the necessary steps to mending a broken relationship. To do so, we are going to use information from Pastor Michael Davis' article titled, "Repairing a Broken Relationship." All information that follows, with the exception of minor bracketed changes, is from his article, which includes some of his personal experiences and gained insight from counseling sessions.

Before we can discuss the process of repairing a relationship, we need to consider what keeps restoration from happening in the first place.

1. *Pride*

I put this one first, because it the biggest and most common obstacle to the healing of relationships. Pride keeps people apart. We know that if we humble ourselves and go to the other person and admit wrong doing, we will lose face- or so we think. I have learned that I lose face by not admitting my error. I save my reputation by swallowing my pride and taking steps to restoration with that person. There is no secret formula to overcoming pride in a broken relationship. We all struggle with it at some point. Simply, you must bite the bullet and go for it. For example, one of the keys to learning to swim is to just go head long into the water and go for it. Too, in a broken friendship, you have to just go for it, do or die.

2. *Time*

Time gets in the way of healing. [T]he longer we wait, the harder it is to take the steps to restore that relationship. [Apostle] Paul wrote to the Christians in

101

Ephesus to "...not let the sun go down while you are still angry,..." (Ephesians 4:26 NIV). That is a good rule to go by. That, in no way, means that you have to fix everything by sunset. It means simply to quickly move into the process of repairing the relationship. The sooner you begin the process of healing the better. Time has a way of desensitizing us, causing us to not see the need for that person like we did when the problem first occurs. Too, as time goes along we can allow bitterness to set in, which exaggerates the problem even more.

3. *Wrong Voices*
We all listen to several voices on a daily basis. The voices can come from advice from people at work, a neighbor or the media. The voices can [also] come from inside us. I am not referring to people who hear voices in an insane kind of way, but rather the voices that crowd our thoughts daily. We must use discernment and not listen to the wrong advice, as that often will lead us to maintain the broken relationship. Obviously, some relationships are not healthy for us to keep, but more often than not we should listen to counsel that encourages us to restore [our broken] relationships.

4. *Unwillingness to Mend the Relationship*
One obstacle that is out of our control is the other person who is unwilling to make amends. That can create more pain for the person who wants badly to restore the [relationship]. [T]he main thing is to be

patient, and give [him/her] space while affirming your love for [him/her].

If after reading through the four listed factors that can interrupt or prolong the process of reconciliation, you find any that pertain specifically to you, you must address the impediment before attempting to take the following steps to repair the broken relationship.

Steps to Repairing the Relationship

1. *Realization of Brokenness*
I put this step first as I am surprised at how many people are oblivious to the broken relationships around them. Often, they do not see that they are a common denominator in a series of broken relationships. If you tend to have relationship problems with several people, take a look at yourself to see if you are the source of the problem.

2. *Humility*
Whether you are the source of the problem or not, humility is a must if the relationship is to be restored. If you are the whole reason for the problem or just a part of it, it takes great humility to admit wrongdoing. The rewards, however, are much greater than the struggle to admit your error.

If you are not the source of the problem, you still must take steps to reconciliation. Do not wait on the other person. It will take humility on your part, especially if you were not the cause of the break with the other person.

3. *Patience*

Patience is necessary. The relationship did not end overnight, so it will not be repaired overnight. You need to give each other time and space to think things through and to heal. Patience is especially necessary if the other person is not willing to reconcile. Don't push [him/her], as that will drive [him/her] further away. Affirm your love for [him/her], respect [his/her] wishes, and allow [him/her] room to figure things out.

4. *Talking Openly*

Talking openly about the problem(s) is a necessary step to healing. This will include a period of blaming, then heart searching, and finally finding a solution.

Blaming is part of the process. We all do it. We blame each other for the problem. This is part of fighting through misunderstandings so that the truth can be found.

Next, we must move into a time of searching ourselves to see where we were wrong. It is extremely rare when only one person is at fault in a broken relationship. More often than not, both parties are guilty. We must search within ourselves to see where we went wrong without justifying ourselves. We must be completely open and honest at this point if wholeness is to be achieved.

Finally, we must move into a serious discussion to find the solution. Phrases such as 'I'm sorry' and other such phrases are not helpful. Genuine seeking of forgiveness and a desire to solve the issues at hand are what bring healing.

5. *Forgiveness*

Forgiveness is so necessary to keep a relationship alive, whether forgiveness is necessary for little or big problems. We must not let bitterness take root, as it will destroy us. Forgiving the other person will be easier if we remember our constant need of forgiveness. We tend not to forgive when we think of ourselves as being better than we really are. We all make mistakes and should forgive as we want to be forgiven. Be generous in your forgiveness.

6. *Practice the Solution*

In a previous step we talked about finding a solution. That is good, as long as we put the solution into practice. For instance, if one of the problems is verbal abuse, then the solution is to use words that build up the other person. That is great, as long as you stop using abusive language and begin to use words that build up. All solutions to problems are only effective if you put them into practice.

Repairing a broken relationship can be very difficult, especially if problems have gone unchecked. However, there is always hope of reconciliation. As time goes along and problems grow it becomes more difficult, but it is still possible to repair the problems if both parties are willing to take the necessary steps.

Never give up hope. Even if the other person is unwilling you must do your part to reconcile without harassing [him/her]. You always want to give [him/her] the space [he/she] needs, while affirming your love. Once the relationship is made whole again, the reward will far outweigh the effort.

Breaking the Chains of
Sickness
and
Disease

Sickness and disease is a result of sin. Is it a direct result of the afflicted person's sin? Not necessarily. You may ask, "How can that be?" or "What does that mean?"

Allow me to explain.

When God created Adam and Eve, the world was free of sin. However, when man ate of the tree of good and evil, after being forbidden to do so by God, sin entered humanity and the earth realm. Adam and Eve freely gave their power over to Satan who is the prince and power of the air. Satan has been given a measure of power. At the same time, we have a tendency to give Satan more power than he actually has a right to. With his power, he afflicts man with various sicknesses, diseases, and debilitating conditions, such as cancer, diabetes, heart disease, ulcers, blindness, strokes, organ failure, tumor growth, substance addictions, and many life-threatening conditions.

Although Satan has a measure of power and uses it to wreak havoc on mankind, God is yet in control. Nothing occurs in our lives without God knowing about it. So you might ask, "Does God allow sickness and disease to exist?" The answer is yes. God gave man free will, the right to make his/her own decisions. However, God clearly states in the Bible in Deuteronomy 30:19 (NKJV), *"I call heaven and earth as witnesses today against you, that I have set before you life and death, blessing and cursing; therefore choose life, that both you and your descendants may live."* Even with these precisely lucid instructions, man does not always choose 'life' and 'blessings.' He often chooses 'death' and 'cursings.' There is a consequence for every choice; there is a reaction for every action.

So, to clarify my earlier statement, the sinful action did not have to necessarily be committed by the afflicted person. But mankind itself committed sin. As a result, all mankind is vulnerable to afflictions. But, I bring you good news! God is able to heal all manner of sickness and disease.

Read the following accounts of two persons whose lives were devastated by an attack of the enemy. See how God prevailed in their lives by healing them of their afflictions.

The first account is Jean Williams' story. Jean is my aunt. She is married to my uncle, who is my mother's brother. Jean is presently 66 years old. Her affliction began 40 years ago. On a recent trip to Chicago, I was able to interview her in person. From the interview, I obtained the following information:

In 1974, Jean, a healthy twenty-six year old wife and mother of one, was a passenger in a car that was traveling along the highway. Suddenly, without warning, Jean and her husband Curtis, who was driving, were involved in a traffic collision. As a result of the impact, Jean abruptly hit her forehead on the dashboard, causing the blood to flush across her face. Following the traffic collision, Jean continued to her job at a local medical center. While there, a physician examined Jean and scheduled her an appointment with a neurologist.

Prior to the scheduled neurological appointment, Curtis and Jean had planned to go to a picnic. Early in the morning, on the day of the picnic, at 5 AM, Jean suffered a Grand Mal seizure. Immediately, Jean was taken to the hospital. The doctors began to investigate the cause of the seizure. After a detailed and thorough investigation, the attending physician discovered a tumor near the main artery in Jean's brain. Not long after, Jean went into surgery and had the tumor partially removed.

After experiencing the seizure and the surgery, life unfortunately did not return to normal. For a period of time, Jean continued to suffer seizures. Then in 1978, Jean's tumor regrew in a different location within her brain. This time, tumor wrapped around the main artery of Jean's brain and was pushing it down. As the surgeon began the operation, he had to slowly cut away the tumor and allow the brain to rise before he continued. The surgery took nearly nine hours but was successful. The surgeon stated that if he had not been able to remove the entire tumor this time she could have been paralyzed, speechless or a vegetable. But thank God, He gave her the victory and called her into the ministry of healing.

During Jean's time of affliction with the brain tumor in 1974 and the tumor in 1978, her responses to her medical condition were different. During her first affliction, Jean was very familiar with the Lord Jesus Christ; however, she had not made Him her personal Lord and Savior. Therefore, she did not seek healing and consolation from Him. However, something was stirred within her, prompting her to read the word of God more than she had in the past. By the time she suffered the second tumor, her relationship with Christ had begun to further develop. That time, her response to the presence of the brain tumor was different from her prior response. She immediately went into prayer and began to seek the Lord for His guidance.

Today, Jean continues to suffer some challenges with memory and other physical issues. However, her challenges are minor and were eventually traced back to the occurrence of rheumatic fever she had suffered as a child. Today, Jean walks with the Lord and has been greatly strengthened by His presence in her life. She now serves in the capacity of a yielded vessel unto the Lord as a minister of the gospel of Jesus Christ. All that she has suffered and been through has not been in vain. The Lord has captured her attention and called her into His service.

Now, she stands as a great testimony for anyone who suffered any kind of medical affliction within his or her physical body. She gives all the glory to Jesus Christ, God the son and Jehovah Rapha, God the father, who heals us.

The second account is Eric Pena's story. Eric is one of my former students and shared his testimony in one of the course essays. After reading his powerful testimony, I acquired his permission to share his story. Eric is presently 44 years old. His deliverance occurred four years ago. His testimony, in his own words, is below:

There is a place out in Shafter, California where people can go if they are plagued by an addiction to drugs and alcohol. It is a Christian Life School that teaches individuals about God and how to live a better life without those things that have brought them such misery. This place is called Teen Challenge. There is a wide variety of men that find their way to the doors of Teen Challenge. They come for both reasons, but ultimately they are all looking for the same thing--a different way of life.

My name is Eric Pena, and in 2010, I was at the end of the line. I went from having a job and a house to letting my own addiction take control over my existence. I found myself living in a tent in a dried up ravine by myself, not knowing what my next step would be. I remember my days being filled with no responsibility. Just being alive seemed to be all there was from one moment to another. I desperately found ways to gather enough money to stay high while attempting to numb myself so that I would not feel anything. This became the only thing that I lived for.

I can recall the day I found myself headed to Teen Challenge. It was so hot outside, and I felt like my brain was on fire right along with every inch of my body. I was so dirty. I could not stand to be around myself much less around others. I had walked from one end of town to the other, literally from the east side to the north side of town. In that particular facility, there were only women housed there. They were outside, and some were watering plants while others were doing other yard work, but they all had happiness about them. It was very noticeable to me.

When one of the women standing there looked up at me, she saw that I was in bad shape and she approached me, asking me if I was hungry or thirsty, which of course I was. She invited me in, gave me food and water, and then proceeded to tell me about the place that I had come to. She told me that it was a place that could help me feel better about myself and give me an opportunity to live life in a different way.

I was introduced to Jesus Christ and told about His life. At the time, I did not want to be part of any church because it wasn't "my thing," yet I realized that any lower for me would ultimately mean death. I weighed my options and decided that I would go until I could get healthy again. I knew that I really wanted to rest, as I was tired and weak. I was given a ride to facility for men located in Shafter, CA. When I arrived, I noticed the men there had that same smile on their faces that caught my eye at the women's home. It was a smile and light they all had that said they were happy individuals.

Upon arriving there, I was given clean clothes, a shower, and the most comfortable bed that I sunk into and slept the most peaceful sleep I had in a long time. That night, I had a peaceful dream of a new life. The next morning, I decided I would stay and see what the place was all about and what it was that drew me to its doors.

It was a different lifestyle than what I was used to, and at times, I felt it was hard. We were required to go on choir outings to different churches that were supportive of the facility. We were required to... yes, you guessed it... sing in front of the congregations, and some individuals gave their own testimony as to how they were being helped by the program. We were also called out to do what they referred to as "work calls," which in essence is a job that we were hired for to earn funds to keep the doors open for others that were suffering as we once were. These consisted of helping individuals move from their residence or clean yards, etc.

One of my favorite things to do was when we would cook a Spaghetti dinner and take it to the homeless on Skid Row in Downtown Los Angeles. This gave us an opportunity to give back to others that were in a situation that we had once found ourselves in. We fed and spoke to them about Teen Challenge letting them know all were welcome.

Do you remember me telling you that I was not into God? Well, I'm not sure when it happened or even how, but all I do know is that I found myself believing. I found myself feeling like there was nothing I could not do. I was praying and asking for help from a God that before I did not know.

I know that on my own I would have never been able to change my life. I was given a place that was safe enough for me to begin learning about my own desires and myself. It is a life-long process, but I am able to do it clear minded. Without a place like Teen Challenge, I know deep in my soul that I would have eventually given in to my addiction and perished in it.

Today, I am 43 years old and will soon be 44. It has been four years since I graduated from the program. As I look back, I know that no matter what life brings across my path, I can stand firm in my beliefs. Knowing that I can pull ahead in life is so freeing and necessary in order to live a life worth living. Life has its ups and downs, but drugs and alcohol are not the answer. What I learned is after the numbing has disappeared, the issues are still there. Learning to deal with life on life's terms is not impossible but in fact is necessary. I found a place called Teen Challenge that gave me the opportunity to start over. For that, I am grateful and continue to move forward in my life because of it.

I am clean and sober today. I have begun my life over, and now I am in College of the Desert as the next step into my future. I do not know how this will turn out, but I will always be grateful to Teen Challenge and praise Jesus Christ through it all. I used to say, "I found Teen Challenge." The truth is- Teen Challenge found me!

Today, like Jean and Eric, you can be healed of whatever may be plaguing you. Follow these five steps and watch God move in your life.

Step One- Activate your faith. The Bible speaks quite frequently on the subject of faith. Hebrews 11:6 tells us, without faith, it is impossible to please God. James 2:26 warns: Faith without works is dead. Faith is defined in the Bible as the substance of things hoped for the evidence of things not seen (Hebrews 11:1). Faith is simply believing something without sense realm evidence. It is believing without seeing. For example, we know we breathe in air, and we are told air is all around us; however, we cannot see it, but yet we believe it exists.

Without faith, we can do nothing. Jesus tells us in St. Luke 17:6 (KJV), *"If ye had faith as a grain of mustard seed, ye might say unto this sycamine tree, Be thou plucked up by the root, and be thou planted in the sea; and it should obey you."* A 'little' faith goes a long way. However, 'much' faith goes a lot further. But 'great' faith will give you miraculous results. Believe that God will heal you, for it is your faith that will move the hand of God.

If you need help to release your faith, look around you and see the miracles that God has already performed. Additionally, the Bible shares several accounts of people being healed from debilitating conditions. One such account is of a woman with an issue of blood.

Luke 8:43-48 (KJV) says: *"And a woman having an issue of blood twelve years, which had spent all her living upon physicians, neither could be healed of any, Came behind him, and touched the border of his garment: and immediately her issue of blood stanched. And Jesus said, Who touched me? When all denied, Peter and they that were with him said, Master, the multitude throng thee and press thee, and sayest thou, Who touched me? And Jesus said, Somebody hath touched me: for I perceive that virtue is gone out of me. And when the woman saw that she was not hid, she came trembling, and falling down before him, she declared unto him before all the people for what cause she had touched him, and how she was healed immediately. And he said unto her, Daughter, be of good comfort: thy faith hath made thee whole; go in peace."*

This woman had great faith, and she believed in Jesus' healing power. She further believed if she could just come in contact with even His clothes, she would be healed from her dreadful condition. The reality is, it was not the touching of His clothes that caused her healing. Rather, it was her faith that caused her healing to be activated in her body.

Now, read the story of the man who was healed from leprosy. Mark 1:40-45 (KJV) states: *"And there came a leper to him, beseeching him, and kneeling down to him, and saying* unto him, *If thou wilt, thou canst make me clean. And Jesus, moved with compassion, put forth his hand, and touched him, and saith unto him, I will; be thou clean. And as soon as he had spoken, immediately the leprosy departed from him, and he was cleansed. And he straitly charged him, and forthwith sent him away; And saith unto him, See thou say nothing to any man: but go thy way, shew thyself to the priest, and offer for thy cleansing those things which Moses commanded, for a testimony unto them. But he went out, and began to publish it much, and to blaze abroad the matter, insomuch that Jesus could no more openly enter into the city, but was without in desert places: and they came to him from every quarter."*

The leper had obviously heard of Jesus and the miracles He had performed. He too desired to be made whole. So, he besought Jesus and made his request known. Philippians 4:6 says, *"Be anxious for nothing, but in everything by prayer and supplication with thanksgiving let your requests be made known to God."* The leper had nothing to lose. So, he took a chance and exercised his faith and demonstrated his belief in the miracle-working power of Jesus. His faith was not in vain!

Next, read the account of the servant who was healed when Jesus simply spoke a word. Matthew 8:5-10 (NIV) says, *"When Jesus had entered Capernaum, a centurion came to him, asking for help. 'Lord,' he said, 'my servant lies at home paralyzed, suffering terribly.' Jesus said to him, 'Shall I come and heal him?' The centurion replied, 'Lord, I do not deserve to have you come under my roof. But just say the word, and my servant will be healed. For I myself am a man under authority, with soldiers under me. I tell this one, "Go," and he goes; and that one, "Come," and he comes. I say to my servant, "Do this," and he does it.' When Jesus heard this, he was amazed and said to those following him, 'Truly I tell you, I have not found anyone in Israel with such great faith.'"* The conversation continues in verse 13: *"Then Jesus said to the centurion, 'Go! Let it be done just as you believed it would.' And his servant was healed at that moment."*

The power of the living God is powerful. His words are powerful and they will accomplish that for which they have been sent. They will not return unto the Lord void (Isaiah 55:11).

If your faith was not already activated, prayerfully after the testimonies that I have included in this chapter and after sharing the testimonies from the word of God, your faith has now been activated to work for you in the area of your own healing. Now that your faith is activated, pray and make your request known unto the Lord.

Step Two- Start praising God. Acknowledge His presence, His sovereignty, His goodness, His grace and mercy, and most of all His healing virtue. God loves worshipers. He loves to be praised, and He inhabits the praises of His people (Psalm 22:3). Remember He is a jealous God, and He demands to be first in our lives. So, give praises unto Him for He is worthy to be praised. The entire book of Psalms is filled with praises unto God and instructions to continually praise Him (i.e. Psalms 147, 150, and 106).

Step Three- Speak to your condition, and command it to go. God has given us power to tread upon serpents and scorpions and nothing by any means should harm us (Luke 10:19). We must use the power we have been given. When we fail to do so, we render ourselves powerless. Think about this, if electrical currents are running through your home, but you fail to turn in the light switch at night, you will remain in the dark. We must use what we have been afforded. If we fail to do so, how can we expect positive results? Satan comes to steal, kill, and destroy, but Jesus came to give us an abundant life (John 10:10). Let's

117

live it. Let's enjoy it. With the power you have, command the affliction to leave your body!

Step Four- Believe you have received your healing. If you believe God and take Him at His word and not doubt you will have what you ask/say. This is an important step in the healing process. If you don't believe the affliction will be expurgated, then why have faith? Once you speak, you must believe. Disbelief will nullify what you say. Read the following account from Matthew 17:14-21:

> *"And when they were come to the multitude, there came to him a certain man, kneeling down to him, and saying, Lord, have mercy on my son: for he is lunatick, and sore vexed: for ofttimes he falleth into the fire, and oft into the water. And I brought him to thy disciples, and they could not cure him. Then Jesus answered and said, O faithless and perverse generation, how long shall I be with you? how long shall I suffer you? bring him hither to me. And Jesus rebuked the devil; and he departed out of him: and the child was cured from that very hour. Then came the disciples to Jesus apart, and said, Why could not we cast him out? And Jesus said unto them, Because of your unbelief: for verily I say unto you, If ye have faith as a grain of mustard seed, ye shall say unto this mountain, Remove hence to yonder place; and it shall remove; and nothing shall be impossible unto you. Howbeit this kind goeth not out but by prayer and fasting."*

On one hand, the disciples must have attempted to rid the boy of his lunacy, but at the same time, they must not have believed they actually had the power to do so. As a result, the boy remained demon possessed until Jesus came and freed him. From this biblical example, we see belief and actions work together. James 2:26 tells us faith without works is dead. Can we also deduce works without faith is also dead?

Step Five- Thank God as you wait for the manifestation of your healing. At this point, you have activated your faith. You have praised God for who He is. You have spoken to your condition and commanded it to go. You have believed the miraculous healing power of God to be manifested in your life. All you need to do now is let God be God and thank Him in advance. He will follow through and do exactly as He said in 3 John 1:2, *"Beloved, I wish above all things that thou mayest prosper and be in health, even as thy soul prospereth."* God wants us to be physically, mentally, emotionally, psychologically, and spiritually healthy.

Conclusion

It was said in a famous movie titled *Forest Gump,* "Life is like a box of chocolates. You never know what you're going to get." When someone gives you a box of assorted chocolates, you may have chocolates that are cherry-filled, solid chocolate all the way through, or chocolate that has caramel and nuts. You never know what is inside the chocolate until you bite into it.

Life is the same way. When a child is born, he or she never knows what lies ahead. However, as he or she begins to grow and experience life, all sorts of triumphs and tragedies have a tendency to occur. The word of God tells us to count it all joy. Does that mean each challenge will be painless. No, it simply means that the joy of the Lord is our strength. As we are faced with divers challenges, we must always keep our focus on the Lord above because He is our deliverer and our strong tower. He will carry us through each and every situation regardless of whether it is abuse, death, unhealthy sexual tendencies, a broken relationship, or sickness and disease. Remember, it was God who allowed the incident to occur, and if He allows us to endure it, He will safely carry us through it.

Remember, prayer is our connection to your heavenly father; therefore, keep focused on your relationship with Him and not on the challenge itself. Women of God, I wish you much love, peace, success, happiness, temperance, and patience in your life as you walk day by day and with strength to face the challenges that may come your way. Remember, the words of our Lord and Savior Jesus Christ, I will not leave you nor will I forsake you. He will be with you every step of the way, so remember to call on His name.

References

All Psychology Centers. "Loss of a Parent." 2013. www.allpsychologycenrers.com

Axelrod, Julie. "The 5 Stages of Loss and Grief" *Psych Central.* 2006. Retrieved July 2014.

Bauer, Fran. "Don't Hurry Grief." *Journal Sentinel.* 1996.

Bernstein Elizabeth. "Delicate Art of Fixing a Broken Friendship" online.wsj.com/news/articles.

Boyd, Richard. *The Impact of Child Sexual Abuse.* Energetics Institute. Perth, West Australia. 2010. http://www.energeticsinstitute.com.au/page/impact_of_chi ldhood_sexual_abuse.html

Davis, Michael. "Repairing a Broken Relationship." 2014.

Dowd, Kathy E. "Vanessa Williams say her molestation made her more sexually promiscuous." 2014.

Gillette, Hope. "What are the physical and emotional health risks of promiscuity?" 2013. http://voxxi.com/2013/01/23/health-risks-of-promiscuity

Lea, Bronwyn. "What God Teaches Us About Broken Marriage Vows." Feb. 27, 2014. www.christianitytoday.com/women/2014/february

Smith, Evelyn R. "Healing hurts by mending fences." *Sunday Gazette.* Aug. 1998.

Ungureanu, Ileana and Jonathan G. Sandberg. "Broken Together." Springer Science+Business Media. 2010.

Gift of Salvation
for
Non-Believers

"For all have sinned, and come short of the glory of God."
Romans 3:23

This section was written especially for non-believers, those who have not accepted the gift of salvation. The gift of salvation saves souls from eternal damnation and is a free gift offered by God himself. John 3:16-18 says, *"For God so loved the world, that he gave his only begotten Son, that whosoever believeth in him should not perish, but have everlasting life. For God sent not his Son into the world to condemn the world; but that the world through him might be saved. He that believeth on him is not condemned: but he that believeth not is condemned already, because he hath not believed in the name of the only begotten Son of God."* This section of scripture tells us God's purpose for giving His son Jesus to the world. The world was in a bad condition. The world was overwrought with sin; the people were living for fleshly desires rather than for God's desires.

As a result of the world's conditions, God decided that He would offer the perfect sacrifice that would save the world from being a place where people were lost and had no hope. He decided that His own son could stand in proxy for the sin-filled world, taking all sin upon Himself.

So Jesus came, born of a virgin, to save this dying world. He walked on this earth for 33 ½ years, doing the work of His Heavenly Father. At the appointed time, He died by way of crucifixion upon a cross at Calvary, on Golgatha's hill. He shed his blood and died for you and for me. Because His blood was pure, it paid the penalty for all unrighteousness and gave those who believe in Him direct access to His father's throne.

Scripture tells us in Matthew 27:51 that the veil of the temple was ripped in two from top to bottom, at the moment that Jesus' spirit left His body. As a result of the veil's removal, we are no longer required to have a high priest make intercession for us. We, as the children of the Most High God, are able to approach the throne God for ourselves, and Jesus sits on the right hand of the Father making intercession for us.

But what is even more miraculous than God offering His own son as the perfect sacrifice was the fact that when Jesus was placed in grave clothes and placed in a tomb, He only remained there until the third day. God would not have it that His son would remain in the heart of the earth forever. In order for people to believe in the awesome power of God and His dear son Jesus, a miracle had to be performed. So, on the third day, after Jesus died on the cross, He was resurrected, demonstrating the omnipotence of God. This very act was the act that would cause people to believe in a god that reigns supreme and holds the power of the universe in His very hands, a god that could save them from themselves.

Today, if you are an unbeliever, you can change your destiny. You can change where you will spend your eternity. Our Heavenly Father gives us the freedom of choice about how we want to live our life here on earth and how we want to spend eternity. In Deuteronomy 30:19, God boldly declares, "*I call heaven and earth to record this day against you, that I have set before you life and death, blessing and cursing: therefore choose life, that both thou and thy seed may live.*"

So, dear friend what choice will you make today? Will you spend your eternity with the Creator or will you suffer Hell's eternal flames? Again, the choice is yours. Just as the men aboard the ship who were with Jonah became believers, you too can make a choice to accept the only one and true living God as your god.

If after reading the above passages, you have decided that you want to spend your eternity in Heaven with God, the creator, and His son Jesus, and the Holy Spirit, read through what has affectionately come to be known as the Roman's Road. This is the road to salvation. As you read through the scriptures that comprise the Roman's Road, you will also read the explanation for each scripture so you will have clarity about what you are reading and confessing.

The Roman's Road to Salvation

The road to salvation begins with Romans 3:23 which declares, *"For all have sinned, and come short of the glory of God."* This scripture explains that everyone has come short of God's glory and needs redemption. Then Romans 6:23a states, *"For the wages of sin is death."* Here, we learn that the consequence of living a life of sin is death. Everyone will experience physical death as a result of the sin committed in the garden of Eden, but those who commit themselves to a life of sin will suffer eternal damnation in the lake of fire (Rev. 19).

Continue with the rest of verse 6:23 that says, *"but the gift of God is eternal life through Jesus Christ our Lord."* There is an alternative to suffering eternal damnation. We can accept the gift of salvation by accepting Jesus as our personal lord and savior. Then, Romans 5:8 says, *"But God commendeth his love toward us, in that, while we were yet sinners, Christ died for us."* We are able to receive the gift of salvation because Christ came to earth and shed His blood for us on the cross.

Continue to Romans 10: 9-10 which says, *"That if thou shalt confess with thy mouth the Lord Jesus, and shalt believe in thine heart that God hath raised him from the dead, thou shalt be saved. For with the heart man believeth unto righteousness; and with the mouth confession is made unto salvation."* If we confess with our mouths that Jesus is the son of God, that he came and died for our sins, and that God raised Him from the dead, we will receive salvation.

Finish with Romans 10:13, which states, *"For whosoever shall call upon the name of the Lord shall be saved."* Call upon the name of God by saying these words, **"Lord Jesus, come into my heart and save me Lord. I believe that you are the Son of God who came and died on the cross for my sins. I believe that you rose from the grave. I also believe that you now sit in heaven on the right side of the Father, making intersession for me. I accept you as my Lord and my Savior."**

Now that you have confessed with your mouth that Jesus is the son of God and that He died for our sins and rose from the grave, **YOU ARE NOW SAVED!!!!** You will spend your eternity in heaven.

The next step is very important- you must find a bible-based church that teaches the word of God and confesses the Lord Jesus Christ to be the son of God. Don't delay. Do this immediately. Do not leave yourself open to the enemy. Get connected with the saints of the Most High God and keep yourself covered with the unspotted blood of the lamb.

Here is my prayer for you.

Father God,

I thank you for the opportunity to minister your word to the unsaved, the unchurched, and the uncommitted. Father God, I pray now for the souls who have just received the gift of salvation. Lord Father, they have opened their hearts to you, and I know that you have received them into your kingdom and written their names in the Book of Life. Father God, I pray that you will touch their lives and show yourself mightily before them. Let their eyes be opened by the scales falling off, allowing them to see clearly.

Father God, I even pray for the backslider, those who have turned away from you after receiving the gift of salvation. You said in your word that you desire that none would perish. So Lord, I send your word to them right now praying that they would confess the iniquity in their heart, repent, and turn from their evil ways, so that they may receive a life of abundance. You said in your word in Matthew Chapter 14, that every knee shall bow before you and every tongue will confess that Jesus is Lord.

Father God, I pray now that we all come under subjection to your word and that we will humbly submit our lives to you. I ask all these things in the name of my Lord and Savior Jesus Christ.

Amen, Amen, Amen!!!!

I will continue to pray for your success in your walk with God. Remember, this spiritual walk that you are about to embark on will not be an easy walk, but remember, the race is not given to the swift but to those who endure to the end.

Be blessed with heaven's best. I love you!

ABOUT THE AUTHOR

Dr. Cassundra White-Elliott resides in California with her family, where as an English/Education professor she works for various community colleges and universities.

When writing, she writes with the direction of the Holy Spirit, in an effort to share with God's people all that He has for them.

In addition to teaching and writing, Dr. White-Elliott also serves as an evangelistic teacher. She is also the founder of International Women's Commission, a ministry that serves the needs of the entire person, by attending to healing the mind, body, soul, and spirit.

Dr. White-Elliott holds a Ph.D. in Education, a Master's in English Composition, and a Bachelor's in Education.

Dr. White-Elliott is also the founder of CLF Publishing, LLC. For your publishing needs, go online to www.clfpublishing.org.

OTHER BOOKS BY THE AUTHOR

(All books can be purchased at

www.creativemindsbookstore.com)

From Despair, through Determination, to Victory!

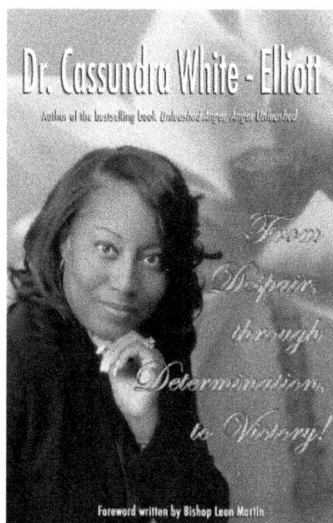

A lot can happen during a span of 40 years. The life of Dr. Cassundra White-Elliott has been anything but uneventful. From a fun-loving childhood sprinkled with incidents of abuse to a tumultuous young adulthood to a stable, secure adult life, she has experienced a full life, with much more to come. Her story is inspiring and motivating.

If anyone lacks hope, reading Dr. White-Elliott's autobiography will propel him/her into an attitude of "Maybe I can." This attitude, if nurtured and developed, will grow into an attitude of "Yes, I can." Throughout her life, Cassundra has always held in her heart the belief that she could achieve anything that she had a made-up mind to embark upon. She was determined to achieve her heart's desires, doing what God has called her to do. She takes no credit for herself. All the glory goes to God, for He is her driving force. In Him, she lives, moves, and has her being.

Through the Storm

Through the Storm was duly inspired by the avaricious cloud of depression that decided to hover overhead of my daily existence in the latter part of 2007. Although I found it extremely difficult, I was once again compelled to not be defeated by just another snare that the enemy, the trickster, set for me. Once again, or more appropriately I should say *continuously*, he has exerted pernicious efforts to snatch the very life out of me by causing me to wallow in despair and to believe that I had been overcome by failure when in actuality and all reality, I was just experiencing a temporary setback. During those cloudy days, I had to remind myself daily that even though I was a target of the enemy, I am and will always be a child of the Most High god, Jehovah, who is my rock, my stability.

Unleashed Anger, Anger Unleashed

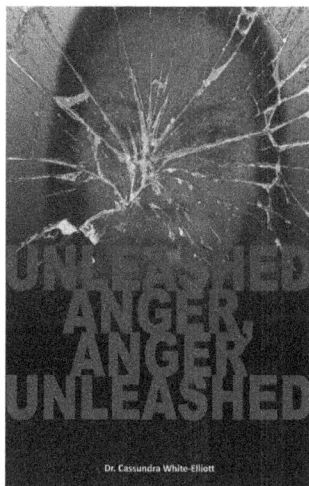

Introduction

What Is This Book All About?

As I prepared to embark upon the adventure of writing this book, I had to prepare myself to also be transparent. I have found that being transparent is required in order for healing to transpire, healing for all those that peruse the pages of this book and myself. And I may as well tell you that today, at the onset of this project, I have not been totally delivered from my condition of being an anger-filled person. However, I am definitely a work in progress. I have made strides with the assistance of my Lord and Savior, Jesus Christ, who is the head of my life. Without his love, guidance, and teachings, I would not be the woman of God I am today. I shudder to think where I could be instead and will therefore not entertain the thought.

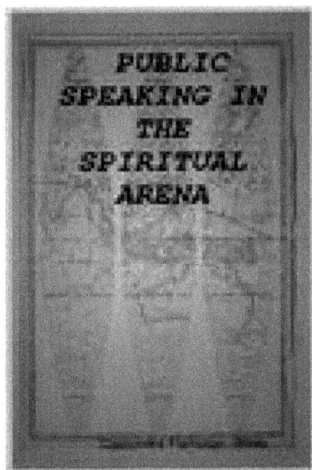

Preview

Chapter Two
How Communication Works

Purpose: This chapter will explain the six primary components of communication, identifying their purpose and how they work together.

The Source

In oral communication, the source of information is the speaker. In a church setting, the foundation of the message is God's word, but it is a speaker's interpretation of God's word that is delivered to the audience. As speakers vary, the information may vary but should have a similar essence because the foundational text is the same.

The Message

The message is the collective set of ideas that the speaker (the source) wants to deliver and/or illustrate to the audience. The message can be informative where the speaker informs the audience about a specific set of information. Or, the message may be persuasive in nature if the speaker wants to persuade the audience about conducting themselves in a specific manner, accepting God's commandments, or any number of things.

Where is Your Joppa?

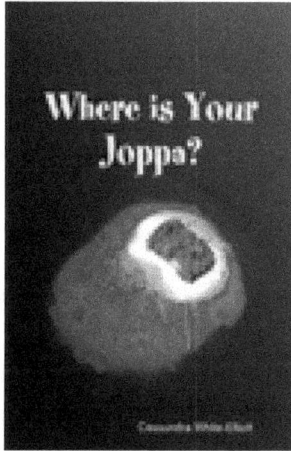

Introduction

Where is Your Joppa? was written for the express purpose of illustrating God's call for obedience in the lives of believers with respect to the individual call that He has on each of our lives. As you read throughout the various chapters, notice that the emphasis is placed on our persistent disobedience in answering God's call in a specific area of our lives. We have become a people who are similar to the Israelites when they found themselves in the middle of the wilderness, following their exodus from Egypt. Before God, they murmured and complained about their current life conditions and failed to be obedient to God's statutes delivered through His servant Moses. Their persistent disobedience caused them to lose the opportunity to see and enter the Promised Land. I ask you, "What has your disobedience cost you?" "Was your disobedience worth what it cost you?" "Do you think about the souls you could have ushered into the kingdom of God?" These are some of the questions that I pray will be answered through your reading of the book.

Mayhem in the Hamptons

Romero and Yolanda optimistically plan for the day that is going to change their lives from being single persons to a couple who is united in holy matrimony. They, along with their parents, close friends and family, fly over to the infamous Hamptons, where only the rich and famous vacation, to have their dream wedding at the five-star Hampton Suites located on a peninsula in the Hamptons. Little do they know that their perfect day will turn out to be less than perfect when their wedding planner Mariesha Coleman suddenly goes missing!

A time when the newlyweds' lives should be filled with joy and the creation of wonderful memories, they are stricken with grief as they desperately try to find clues to help solve Mariesha's disappearance.

Mayhem in the Hamptons is a tale that shares how the horrors of a woman's past can come back to haunt her in more than one way and the impact it can have on anyone who gets in the way.

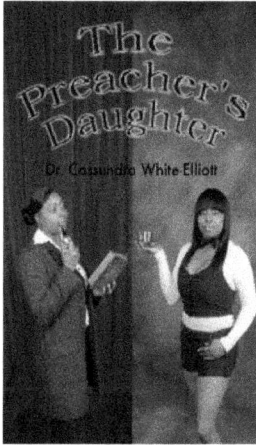

Tinisha, the daughter of a preacher, is a twenty-six year old God-fearing young woman endeavoring to complete law school so that she can make her mark in the courtroom. Working in one of the late-night clubs in Hollywood to earn money to pay her own way through school, Tinisha soon learns that life doesn't always go as planned. Finding her strength in her faith, Tinisha constantly finds herself praying as she watches God move miraculously in her life.

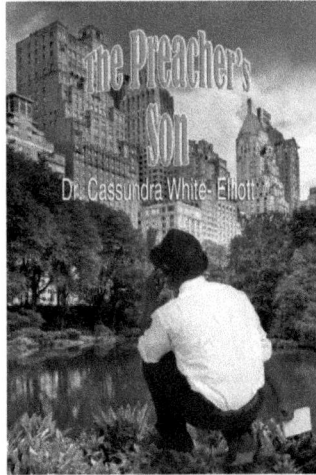

Romero Turner is a private investigator with a promising future. As he continues to build his career, he is excited about the cases he undertakes. However, his father Pastor Theodore Turner has other plans for his son's life. In the midst of trying to save his client's husband from Sylvester Domingo, a ruthless crime lord, Romero must try to salvage his relationship with his father. He must decide if ministry or life as a detective is in his future.

Lord, Teach Me to be a Blessing!

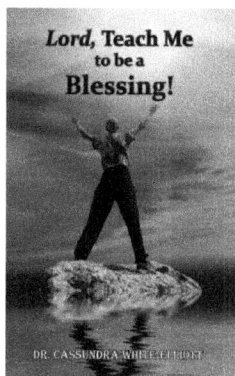

Lord, Teach Me to be a Blessing! will change a person's mentality from being centered around "me, myself, and I" to focusing on "others."

The world system teaches us that it is acceptable to place ourselves above others in an attempt to get ahead and even to survive. Herbert Spencer coined the phrase *'survival of the fittest'* after reading Charles Darwin's theory of evolution. This concept of surpassing and outdoing others is the world's philosophy.

However, the word of God does not subscribe to or promote this self-centered ideology, and therefore, neither should believers. We must hold fast to the truths outlined in Holy Scripture: *"Love thy neighbor as you love thyself"* (James 2:8) and *"It is more blessed to give than to receive"* (Acts 20:35).

While holding God's truths to be self-evident, we must demonstrate them to others, thereby showing them the way of the Lord of how to be a blessing to someone *rather* than looking to receive a blessing.

This is the very purpose of this book: to change the mentality of the world from being *self*-centered to *other* centered.

After the Dust Settles

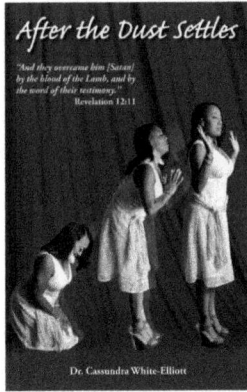

Throughout the journey of life, we all experience ups and downs and joys and pains. Most of us successfully find solutions to the situations/problems we encounter, but we often avoid dealing with the attached emotions. If we continue to ignore the emotions of pain, hurt, disappointment, anger, etc., we set ourselves up for destruction. Our families, our cultures, and our society tell us to be strong, to keep our chin up, and to grin and bear it. However, these methods of avoidance can lead us to strokes due to the undue amount of pressure we place on ourselves and/or mental illness from being unable to cope with the emotional baggage we have accumulated.

In *After the Dust Settles,* Dr. C. White-Elliott shares several situations that we all may encounter at one time or another in our lifetime and how to successfully navigate through them, so we can find ourselves emotionally healthy after the dust has settled and the situation has been rectified.

Begin reading today and experience a better tomorrow!

A Diamond in the Rough

A Diamond in the Rough Architecture Firm was built and is owned and operated by lead architect Kyra Fraser. For the last five years, Kyra has been extremely successful in business, but her love life leaves much to be desired.

Kyra has set high standards for herself and does not wish to take a man in any condition and attempt to make him over. She is looking for someone who is drama free, well educated, very cultured, fun-loving, good looking, self-motivated, and the list goes on.

Will Kyra find the man of her dreams, or will her dream just continue to be a dream?

As you delve into this page-turning novel, Kyra's reality will unfold as you are drawn into her world of design, love and office drama- which includes her best friend's husband who is looking for love in all the wrong places.

365 Days of Encouragement

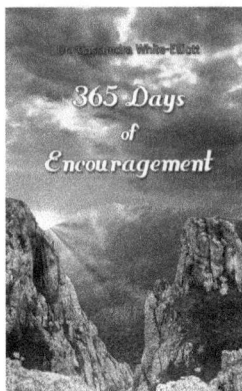

Just as our brain requires oxygen obtained from the air we breathe to sustain our mortal bodies, our spirit requires revitalization and encouragement in order to be strengthened each and every day of our lives. The revitalization and encouragement needed for the spirit of man comes directly from the word of God and assists us in walking according to the way of our heavenly Father. 365 Days of Encouragement provides a scripture a day for each day of the year. Along with the daily scripture is a brief note of commentary also for the benefit of edifying the saints of God.

It is my prayer that the people of God would live a fulfilled life through Christ Jesus. Knowing His word and understanding we can walk in the fulfillment thereof is empowering. We are instructed in II Timothy 2:15, "Study to shew thyself approved unto God, a workman that needeth not to be ashamed, rightly dividing the word of truth" (KJV). Take an opportunity to delve further into the word of God, to know His statutes and to allow your own personal life to be edified, so you can be equipped to bring glory to God and lived a fulfilled life.

A Mother's Heart

A Mother's Heart shares the unconditional love of mothers through a compilation of testimonies. Each testimony serves as a tribute to a special mother. The children of the represented mothers have lovingly written about their childhood, young adult life and/or older adult experiences they shared with their mother. As you read the writers' reflections, you will feel the expressions of love exude from the pages.

The purpose of this book is two-fold. First, it honors those mothers who stood by their children through the trials of life and showered them with unconditional love. Second, the book is a source of encouragement for mothers who may feel inadequate and question whether or not they are actually suited for motherhood. Our advice to mothers is, "Be encouraged; the journey of motherhood may seem daunting at times and you may shed some tears, but your children will never forget the love you have shown them and instilled in them to share with others."

Mothers may not be perfect, but they are definitely unmatched by any other category of person on God's green earth!